Tracing Your Prisoner Ancestors

FAMILY HISTORY FROM PEN & SWORD BOOKS

Birth, Marriage & Death Records
The Family History Web Directory
Tracing British Battalions on the Somme
Tracing Great War Ancestors
Tracing History Through Title Deeds
Tracing Secret Service Ancestors
Tracing the Rifle Volunteers
Tracing Your Air Force Ancestors
Tracing Your Ancestors
Tracing Your Ancestors from 1066 to 1837
Tracing Your Ancestors Through Death Records – Second Edition
Tracing Your Ancestors through Family Photographs
Tracing Your Ancestors Through Letters and Personal Writings
Tracing Your Ancestors Using DNA
Tracing Your Ancestors Using the Census
Tracing Your Ancestors: Cambridgeshire, Essex, Norfolk and Suffolk
Tracing Your Aristocratic Ancestors
Tracing Your Army Ancestors
Tracing Your Army Ancestors – Third Edition
Tracing Your Birmingham Ancestors
Tracing Your Black Country Ancestors
Tracing Your Boer War Ancestors
Tracing Your British Indian Ancestors
Tracing Your Canal Ancestors
Tracing Your Channel Islands Ancestors
Tracing Your Church of England Ancestors
Tracing Your Criminal Ancestors
Tracing Your Docker Ancestors
Tracing Your East Anglian Ancestors
Tracing Your East End Ancestors
Tracing Your Family History on the Internet
Tracing Your Female Ancestors
Tracing Your First World War Ancestors
Tracing Your Freemason, Friendly Society and Trade Union Ancestors
Tracing Your Georgian Ancestors, 1714–1837
Tracing Your Glasgow Ancestors
Tracing Your Great War Ancestors: The Gallipoli Campaign
Tracing Your Great War Ancestors: The Somme
Tracing Your Great War Ancestors: Ypres
Tracing Your Huguenot Ancestors
Tracing Your Insolvent Ancestors
Tracing Your Irish Family History on the Internet
Tracing Your Jewish Ancestors
Tracing Your Jewish Ancestors – Second Edition
Tracing Your Labour Movement Ancestors
Tracing Your Legal Ancestors
Tracing Your Liverpool Ancestors
Tracing Your Liverpool Ancestors – Second Edition
Tracing Your London Ancestors
Tracing Your Medical Ancestors
Tracing Your Merchant Navy Ancestors
Tracing Your Northern Ancestors
Tracing Your Northern Irish Ancestors
Tracing Your Northern Irish Ancestors – Second Edition
Tracing Your Oxfordshire Ancestors
Tracing Your Pauper Ancestors
Tracing Your Police Ancestors
Tracing Your Potteries Ancestors
Tracing Your Pre-Victorian Ancestors
Tracing Your Prisoner of War Ancestors: The First World War
Tracing Your Railway Ancestors
Tracing Your Roman Catholic Ancestors
Tracing Your Royal Marine Ancestors
Tracing Your Rural Ancestors
Tracing Your Scottish Ancestors
Tracing Your Second World War Ancestors
Tracing Your Servant Ancestors
Tracing Your Service Women Ancestors
Tracing Your Shipbuilding Ancestors
Tracing Your Tank Ancestors
Tracing Your Textile Ancestors
Tracing Your Twentieth-Century Ancestors
Tracing Your Welsh Ancestors
Tracing Your West Country Ancestors
Tracing Your Yorkshire Ancestors
Writing Your Family History
Your Irish Ancestors

TRACING YOUR PRISONER ANCESTORS

A Guide for Family Historians

STEPHEN WADE

Pen & Sword
FAMILY HISTORY

First published in Great Britain in 2020 by
PEN & SWORD FAMILY HISTORY
An imprint of
Pen & Sword Books Limited
Yorkshire - Philadelphia

Copyright © Stephen Wade, 2020

ISBN 978 1 52677 8 529

The right of Stephen Wade to be identified as Author of this work has been asserted by him in accordance with the Copyright, Designs and Patents Act 1988.

A CIP catalogue record for this book is available from the British Library

All rights reserved. No part of this book may be reproduced or transmitted in any form or by any means, electronic or mechanical including photocopying, recording or by any information storage and retrieval system, without permission from the Publisher in writing.

Typeset by Mac Style
Printed and bound in the UK by CPI Group (UK) Ltd,
Croydon, CR0 4YY

Pen & Sword Books Limited incorporates the imprints of Atlas, Archaeology, Aviation, Discovery, Family History, Fiction, History, Maritime, Military, Military Classics, Politics, Select, Transport, True Crime, Air World, Frontline Publishing, Leo Cooper, Remember When, Seaforth Publishing, The Praetorian Press, Wharncliffe Local History, Wharncliffe Transport, Wharncliffe True Crime and White Owl.

For a complete list of Pen & Sword titles please contact
PEN & SWORD BOOKS LIMITED
47 Church Street, Barnsley, South Yorkshire S70 2AS, United Kingdom
E-mail: enquiries@pen-and-sword.co.uk
Website: www.pen-and-sword.co.uk
Or
PEN AND SWORD BOOKS
1950 Lawrence Rd, Havertown, PA 19083, USA
E-mail: Uspen-and-sword@casematepublishers.com
Website: www.penandswordbooks.com

CONTENTS

Acknowledgements vi

How to Use this Book vii

Introduction xi

   Chapter 1   The History of Prisons in Britain I 1

   Chapter 2   The History of Prisons in Britain II 15

   Chapter 3   Staff and the Regime 25

   Chapter 4   Prison Records I 36

   Chapter 5   Prison Records II 50

   Chapter 6   Prison Records III 63

   Chapter 7   Transportation 75

   Chapter 8   Criminal Lunatics 89

   Chapter 9   Secondary Records 99

   Chapter 10 Contemporary Sources in Print/Online 113

   Chapter 11 Criminal Offences 136

Bibliography and Sources 162

Index 175

ACKNOWLEDGEMENTS

As usual with historical works, the research project always needs plenty of expert help. In this case, I give special thanks to the staff at the Lincolnshire Archives and the East Riding Archives. Looking at prison history demands a great deal of diverse material, and often the most relevant documentary sources are seemingly, at the initial stage, peripheral. With these complications in mind, thanks go to Keiley McCartney and Simone Baddeley in particular, at Lincolnshire Archives, and to Sarah Acton and Helen Clark in Beverley.

Researching prisons is notoriously difficult, largely because so many records have disappeared, but also because so many are closed, for political reasons. Countless editors and specialists have helped with understanding such records. We have to work with what we have.

There always momentous works of scholarship behind any work seeking to offer a general, readable account of a strand of social history. In this case, the works in question are by David T. Hawkings (on genealogy) and also Norval Morris and David Rothman (on prison history). I owe a debt to those writers in that their work provides a platform for all historians working this seam. (See the Bibliography for details of their books).

Thanks also go to my editor at Pen & Sword, Amy Jordan, who has been patient with regard to my appeals for help and advice.

For all kinds of help and consultation, thanks go to genealogist Barbara Schenck, who always gives help where it is needed, and to Brian Elliott, my first editor in the genre of crime history.

HOW TO USE THIS BOOK

Every work of genealogy, if it aims at being a general guide, has to cover a multitude of sources of information; these will differ from mainstream material to a scattering of mixed sources. The latter will offer nothing more than a time-consuming search with a vague hope that something may turn up. But at least in the mainstream documents there are always 'leads'.

My experience in this area of criminal history has shown me that in order to find information about an ancestor beyond the expected trajectory of the life events, there has to be a mix of optimism and serendipity. To use this book profitably, therefore, it is wisest to be satisfied with the central spine of the prison narrative, which may be outlined in this way:

- A search with the name across a certain timespan
- A look at the primary court records
- A search of prison registers and calendars
- A timespan search across secondary sources

Any historical study will be a desperate work of retrieval, a determined effort to arrive somewhere near the truth, knowing that the truth is actually impossible to find and define. When it comes to crime history, and the machinations of the great law engine, driving through society as the historical process relentlessly unfolds, the facts of a transgression are never simple and always challenging. This is because an offence is caught up in the *mores* and values of a specific time; we see the accused trapped in a web of law like a fly at the mercy of a spider. When prison enters the narrative, the net has closed.

The word 'tracing' implies detective work, and so it is. The majority of prison records we have to deal with date from the Industrial Revolution of c.1760–1830, and the second wave of Empire, through to the First World War. In those years, the acceleration in population increase makes the detective work required to find Jim Smith, who stole a horse, or Jane Jones, who cashed a fraudulent cheque, more involved. Many records have been lost and dispersed, often into secondary sources outside the main criminal justice system records.

Major villains, such as the bank robbers, the multiple killers, the poisoners, baby-farmers and pirates, stand out. Their horrendous offences generate multi-textured stories with ups and downs. There is finality, and a definite, clear paper trail. But the petty thief, or the poor young woman who conceals a birth, become figures in a long list of many little-known people in a mass population.

Tracing Your Prisoner Ancestors offers some help amid all this material, and against the confusions and perplexities of penal systems. The focus is on prison and prison records, but I have had to build in some explanations of the legal processes involved in prosecution, arrest and detention. Concepts of prison and what it is for have changed in cycles of ideologies, powered by governments and theorists with varying notions of what prison is for. But at bottom there have always been two fundamental questions about incarceration. First, does prison work? That question always has provisos and qualifications. Second, what is prison for? It has always been for punishment, or at least for detention until law moves forward. But from the twentieth century onwards, with the advent of sophisticated policing and forensic knowledge, along with mass and serial murders, terrorism and world wars, the answers to these two basic questions have become more and more muddled, run through with moral dilemmas, and with political dimensions.

With all this in mind, using this book for family history research will present the reader with a certain common ground of familiar criminal offences and there will be limitations. As well as the state prison systems in the mainstream of criminal law, there are peripheral court functions, and these have run through British history. Many of these courts entail elements of prisoner information. A perfect instance of this is the Court of Criminal Appeal, which was first functioning in 1907. I have included these marginal sources in the last two chapters. These records all refer to prisoners, and the hearings give us an insight into the initial trial of our ancestor, not found elsewhere.

Approaching prison history in general, as distinct from tracing prisoners from the past, is a tough challenge for the researcher. The reasons for this are numerous, but the principal reason is that some records have been lost, and those which do survive, from the early years of prison history in Britain, tend to give only basic information.

It is hard to go beyond the bare bones of a standard document. Sometimes, the information contained on a calendar of prisoners, which lists the inmates at a particular time, is all the historian is able to locate.

For this reason, my book offers substantial secondary material. Using these sources is time-consuming, but is often the only option if a writer genuinely wants to know more about their ancestor's life behind bars.

I recommend the following steps to maximise the usefulness of this book:

- First, try to find the standard prison documentation, as described here.
- Second, search for the main secondary material (such as doctors' or matrons' journals for instance). A sweep through entries for a given span of dates will help.
- Third, search newspaper reports for a set period.
- Finally, check published material such as reports, memoirs and official publications.

From experience, I would say that often by sheer persistence and serendipity, you will find that your prisoner's experience will relate to something of the time, the period under scrutiny. I have given ample space to explaining historical context in the case studies I have mentioned or summarised. For instance, during the mid to late Victorian period there were dozens of parliamentary enquiries and reports on prisons, and many of these deal with individual gaols. In some cases, the reports even contain material such as plans and statistical tables relating to certain institutions.

The other main element in researching prisoners from the past is the necessary effort to find the 'flow' of an individual convict's life and experience. By this I mean that in most cases, the string of institutions of a secondary nature will probably yield more information on your ancestor. In practical terms this means that in many cases, the man who is living in his cell in a local or convict gaol c.1880 will in all likelihood have been a juvenile offender. He may have been resident in a workhouse or in a reformatory. The initial newspaper search will be likely to find brief reports on petty offences, particularly from mid-Victorian times, when the police courts started to take over much of the work done by regional magistrates.

One of the delights of this area of research is the locating of a small localised incident in the bigger picture (referred to by historians as the *metanarrative* of a time or period). My own most memorable experience of this was when I was looking for the destination of a Doncaster man who had killed his wife while he was extremely drunk. I found out which prisons he went to, and once I knew he served some time in Dartmoor, I looked for memoirs of that prison. Luck was on my side: a famous Irish Republican radical was in Dartmoor at the same time as my man, and they met. This meeting went into the Irishman's published memoir.

To summarize, then, the most successful procedure is to build upwards from the basic prison records. The most thorough and extensive of these records is the nominal record (discussed further in Chapter 4). This gives a mass of information, ranging from height/weight to 'degree of education' and distinctive physical features.

I have devoted the first three chapters to explanations of the history of our prisons, and of what existed before we had anything resembling a prison *system*. This is essential material for the researcher, because although main cases and trials from the late seventeenth century are often included in the *Annual Register* or online at the Old Bailey Sessions Papers site, the vast number of prisoners who were tried and convicted out in the provinces, or at the thrice yearly assizes, may only be found and studied in the papers available at our local archives. The *Annual Register* was a publication that covered court trials, and it provides an excellent source for assizes.

Fortunately, it is now a simple matter to access British newspapers online, and this resource covers a large proportion of the regional newspapers up to 1950. After that we now have other newsprint resources.

Finally, a useful guideline to bear in mind is the fact that riots, disasters, robberies and murders are a marvellous resource for the crime researcher. This is because major crime tends to attract the press and other media, and names of only secondary interest are often listed. A case in point is the 1811–12 Luddite risings in West Yorkshire. This was a case of war in the streets and in the mills, and the militia were called out. As a result, many of the leaders of this violence and criminal damage were tried and hanged at York. In the trial reports, many other people have a mention. Ancestors may have been there, though they may not have been major players.

Equally, the changing prison systems through time may also throw up anomalies and surprises. For instance, a Hansard report in 1967 revealed the case of a 15-year-old boy who, it had been discovered, had been kept with the adults in Lincoln prison. Apparently he was awaiting a place in Borstal. But that represents yet another instance of an ancestor being hard to trace because of the current system and anomalous provision.

INTRODUCTION

Understanding prison

As long as there have been prisons in human societies, there has been the question: how is it that a minority of people can keep order and control of a very large number? How is it that a huge prison population, such as the 1,000+ inmates of the modern super-jail, may be regulated and suppressed by authority? There have been prisons of one kind or another as long as there have been unacceptable transgressions or, of course, as long as there have been wars, as wars entail dealing with enemies.

The point about wars leads to another central question about prisons: how have they learned to deal with criminals as well as with political inmates? The instances from history which might provide some answers are often confusing. The *Mayflower* Pilgrims, for example, were 'held' in cells at Boston, Lincolnshire during their efforts to form a radical religious community. They were not technically 'imprisoned'.

History provides some answers to such questions, but they reflect more on the contemporary society than on any philosophy of what prison should be. Every age has its *Zeitgeist*, its spirit, expressed in its ideologies and in its political structures. As a broad generalisation, it could be argued that when a society is comfortable with itself, its jails are considered and noticed; when the society is fearful, guarded, paranoid even, its prisons become repositories for the 'underclass'.

Unfortunately, in British history the history of prisons reflects the predominance of a view of prison as oblivion rather than as treatment and care. A criminal is deprived of his or her liberty. That is the base punishment of a prison sentence. The individual is kept in a locked box; they have only the restricted freedom allowed by the prison guards. On top of that, everything else that happens inside the prison walls is open to discussion. It becomes, in our history, a 'regime'. That is the word employed in the context. A governor and staff enforce that regime, daily and with a method. The method is explained in published prison rules. In Britain post-Enlightenment (arguably by the 1830s) a prison is supposed to be a place that delivers care and treatment, once freedom has been deprived.

For other periods, such as the Tudor years for instance, torture was part of the prison regime: it was all about suffering as well as the deprivation of freedom. In classical times, imprisonment was a limbo, in which the unfortunate victim was either simply shut away, or perhaps, with a possibility of ransom, he or she was preserved as an asset. The great Spanish writer, Miguel de Cervantes, author of *Don Quixote*, was captured by the Turks and was ransomed by his brother.

In modern periods, with the arrival of the penitentiary, the fundamental change in attitudes concerned the possibility that a miscreant (and sinner) could or would be returned to society, or at least returned to a state in which his sins could be expiated. The Victorians saw the value of such attitudes, and the influence of the Evangelical movement had an impact there. In 1846 the Evangelical Alliance was created, setting its beliefs opposite to 'Romanism' and the rational mind; then in the 1860s the movement grew apace, as may be seen by the establishment in 1865 of the Christian mission, as William Booth put it, 'for the evangelisation of the very lowest classes'. Also, there was the London Mission of 1842. The affirmation that reform and redemption were possible in good works had an impact on criminological thought.

A more practical dimension on understanding prison is to absorb the attitudes to crime at the time of our ancestor's incarceration. For example, the nineteenth-century decrease in offences against the person, as 'white collar' offences increased. By the mid-nineteenth century, the Industrial Revolution was arguably in a second phase, and the new towns and commercial enterprise the changes engendered brought an expansion of clerical and administrative work: the civil service grew and all businesses demanded more office staff. There was growth in the numbers of commuters living in the London suburbs and travelling into the city for work.

In turn, offences related to the many varieties of fraud became more common: embezzlement, forgery, larceny and various kinds of 'cooking the books' emerged. The first ever 'true crime' story on film came about after the infamous Liverpool Goudie fraud in which a clerk embezzled his employers. This was in 1901, when film-makers Mitchell and Kennedy made *The Arrest of Goudie*.

The other factor which needs to be grasped is that of prison staff. In the first local gaols and bridewells, staff were often family and everything was handled locally. Sons and daughters were often brought up to work in the prison administration run by their managerial parents. Then a gradual change occurred, and the records from the mid-nineteenth century show the establishment of officers – the warders and wardresses. In memoirs of convict prisoners from the late Victorian to the Edwardian period we see much evidence of the nature of this new breed of officer. These professionals really come to light in the period of the Suffragette radical movement in the Edwardian era and early years of George V. Suffragettes were educated women, and many wrote memoirs or were featured in the press. They usually mentioned and described the staff inside the prison walls.

Between the world wars, there were innovative attempts at prison reform, and prison staff tended to be mentioned in press reports. For the Victorian period, and for the earlier Georgian era, information regarding staff tends to be in parliamentary reports and state papers. Often, in prison enquiries and reports, transcripts of interviews with officers are included in the printed materials.

Finally, there is the subject of sources: the internet has brought so many source materials online and easily accessed that much more may be achieved while simply sitting at a desk at home, than when, in quite recent times, this research entailed delving into a number of physical archives. However, actual paper archives, stored at the county record office, often include numbers of secondary items, most of which will not have been digitalised.

An example from my own research illustrates the way in which a batch of documents often leads, laterally, to more information than can be found online. In the process of researching the 1852 Ireland's Eye case (which is infamous in Ireland and has spawned several book-length studies), I came across a cross-reference: something which did not pertain to the mainstream prison records. It was new information, and very significant, as it was a bundle of Home Office papers relating to appeals and letters asking for clemency. They formed part of a bundle based on the colony of Bermuda, and they represented an area of the case which had been little studied (see Bibliography under Wade, Stephen).

Overall, reports of prisons in the past have entailed some shocks and surprises: prison life tends to attract incidents and scandals, outrages and abuses. For this reason, the media have always taken an interest in penal policy and efforts at reform. This is always of great assistance in research.

Scope and limitations

I have touched on the limitations of research into prisoner ancestors already, but before I offer further explanation it is useful to define the scope of the book. As soon as a family historian does a survey of records involved in an enquiry, the fact that the scope is restricted by the accessibility of the mainstream material becomes evident. For instance, before the first house of correction in the 1550s (in London at Bridewell), most records relating to prisoners referred to manors and parishes; that is to say that before a central system of gaols was established, being a 'prisoner' meant that a person was awaiting a trial. This could mean that they were held somewhere. The options were many and varied, from the cells at the Boston Guildhall where the *Mayflower* Pilgrims were held for some time, to the dungeon at York Castle.

There were courts of many kinds, run by the church as well as by the manorial officials, long before the houses of correction. The watersheds of the important turning-points in the history of our prisons impose the scope of the present project. These moments in penal history are: the 1550s and the houses of correction; the Gaol Acts of the 1820s, under Robert Peel's reforms; and the 1877 reorganisation of the prisons into local and convict categories.

Yet matters do not end there. Prisons also encompassed military establishments and debtors' prisons for much of the time period we have to cover most thoroughly. On top of this, from the early seventeenth century through to the 1850s Britain had a system of transportation to the colonies in operation, and this generates yet more prison records, such as those relating to the use of prison hulks on the River Thames.

Thus the scope of this book is very wide indeed, as I attempt to include these byways off the mainstream records. We have to accept that as pre-1700 sources present many difficulties, there will be frustrations. One factor here is that some records are written in Latin. In addition, of course, there is the problem of handwriting: so often, texts from earlier centuries present the modern reader with a demanding read.

I have tried to give a fair amount of background information. This is based on the notion that knowing about the prison where your ancestor was kept, along with the forces that acted on that prison regime, will provide a context which will make it easier to envisage the human perspective on the imprisonment.

With these factors in mind, it is clear that the scope of the book is to offer a detailed account of the main period of written records, together with a rather sketchy look at the earlier records. It will become clear that pre-1700 there is a diversity of sources available, but they are piecemeal, and not always easy to use.

Any prison regime will necessarily entail the control and management of the many by the few. For this to function well, there has to be a degree of suppression; mediaeval and Reformation penal provision saw no need to record the consequences of such hard-line management. Later, when every action inside prison walls brought some kind of reaction, record-keeping became important.

There will always be limitations in a book such as this. I have had to limit the space given to explaining the more theoretical aspects of penology. I strongly recommend perusing John Howard's prison reports (see Bibliography) in order to understand the nature of eighteenth-century prison regimes.

The nature of documentation

The documents for research into prisoners' lives have a number of drawbacks and present some difficulties. Often, the real search for the life and actions of an ancestor will begin with something like this, from Richard Gough's classic account of the Shropshire parish of Myddle (1701):

> *We have not mentioned here how we set his son twice apprentice and how he outrun both his masters, we lost our money and he was put in the house of Correction.*

What this tells us is that so much in prison records depends on understanding the beginnings of the person's offence and its context. In this case, the note is all about the parish council and the petty session's attempts to help a local transgressor.

A grasp of the trial and court process will help the reader see the beginnings of a criminal career, and when it comes to trials and courts, British history presents far more than the magistrate's bench up to the assizes. For instance, in John Evelyn's diaries, we have this entry for 1702–03:

> *News of Vice-Admiral Benbow's conflict with the French fleet in the West Indies in which he gradually behaved himself, and was wounded, and would have had extraordinary success had not four of his men-of-war stood spectators without coming to his assistance; for this, two of their commanders were tried by a council of war and executed; a third was condemned to perpetual imprisonment, loss of pay and incapacity to serve in future. The fourth died.*

The men in question were prisoners, but it is hard to imagine the demands of a search into the story of the prisoners referred to. The Admiralty, like the church, had its own courts.

The documentation for this area of history is, therefore, reliable and factually sound in the central spine documents, but beyond these, there is a huge demand on our time and our determination.

There have been other influences on what materials lie in the county archives. Of course, keeping the sheer mass of records from a prison is a logistical challenge. Governments have tried to play a part in sorting and dealing with the storage of such materials. In 1995, for instance, an Instruction to Governors was issued on record management, and this

ORIGIN AND OUTLINE

OF THE

PENITENTIARY SYSTEM

IN

The United States of North America,

TRANSLATED AND ABRIDGED

FROM THE FRENCH OFFICIAL REPORT

OF

Messrs. G. de BEAUMONT & A. de TOCQUEVILLE.

BY WILLIAM B. SARSFIELD TAYLOR,

Hon. Sec. to the Society for Diffusing Information upon Capital Punishments.

London:
SOLD BY J. & A. ARCH, CORNHILL;
LONGMAN, REES, ORME, BROWN, AND GREEN, PATERNOSTER-ROW;
J. HATCHARD AND SON, PICCADILLY; TREUTTEL, WURTZ, AND CO., SOHO-SQUARE;
D. LIZARS, EDINBURGH; AND R. M. TIMS, DUBLIN.

1833.

Frontispiece for William Taylor's book on the penitentiary system. (Author)

was the point at which records were directed to be transferred from the prison estates to the county records office. The governors had to submit records to the local archivist and then:

> *The local archivist should produce a list of the records he/she wants to take, together with details of when they can be made available to the public.*

This applied to records over thirty years old. But there was one problematic statement in this paper: 'There is no need to keep records more than 30 years old which are of no historical interest …' Again, it was supposed to be down to the archivist to decide what the phrase 'no historical interest' could mean as a guide to the sifting process of dealing with records.

Influential thinkers and the concept of prison

Before beginning the chapters on the history of prisons, it is worth looking at the main influential ideas about prison which have affected British penal policy, and the thinkers and politicians who were involved in prison ideologies and reform. These ideas ranged from matters relating to punishment and retribution in earlier times, but in the eighteenth century, which included the years we now refer to as the Enlightenment, notions of atonement, self-reflection and rehabilitation began to emerge. More humanitarian views slowly began to have an impact on how governments saw prison and its purposes.

Enlightenment thinking percolated down from theorists to the actual implementation of imprisonment. By the last decades of the eighteenth century there was more awareness of the limitations of simply punishing or removing (by transportation mainly) society's offenders. Arguably the first important step forward in penal thinking was Cesare Beccaria's work, *Of Crimes and Punishment*, which appeared in 1763.

Beccaria and others were beginning to see that justice needed to be more equitable and well considered, and within the courts and the criminal justice systems of Europe new attitudes began to take root. Around the same time, some events involving gaols began to hit the headlines. There were scandals about inequality in prisons, with different treatment being meted out to the rich and the poor. Abuse of power became pressing business for parliamentary and legal reformers.

One important figure in these early years of revising the philosophies behind incarceration was Sir George Onesiphorus Paul, a Gloucestershire JP. He and some friends established a penitentiary in 1792 and this turned out to be a visionary experiment. As prison historians Elizabeth Newbury and Tim Wood explain:

The prison was built in three parts with a jail for felons awaiting trial, a house of correction for minor offenders, and a penitentiary house which contained a honeycomb of cells (52 night cells and 52 day cells) and several secure exercise yards. (from Punishment and Prisons – see Bibliography)

At this time, there had been no thought given to mixing all categories of prisoners under the same roof and in the prison grounds.

Understanding prison lives

Before embarking on research into your prisoner ancestor, it is useful to have some knowledge of the thinking behind British prisons throughout the centuries. For much of the time between the first houses of correction and the establishment of the modern prison estate, philosophies of prison sentences have fluctuated between retribution and rehabilitation. Different attitudes tend to come and go in a cyclical way, as governments and criminological ideas change.

But in whatever period your ancestor served his or her time, some fundamental aspects of prison life need to be considered:

a) A prison stretch always involves some kind of 'purposeful activity' unless some factors of control interfere.
b) There is always the question of what the Victorians called 'contamination', when a first-time offender may be influenced by a recidivist.
c) Categories of inmate have differed over time. For example, on many occasions, the issues affecting individual prisoners have been related to whether or not they have been defined as political prisoners. This marked them out from the 'common criminal' inside. Equally, for centuries there were convicted criminals under the same roof as debtors. Further complications arise when we consider that for a long time prisoners awaiting trial (what we today call 'on remand') mixed with convicted criminals.
d) There are social aspects to prison sentences, which will emerge during research. Inmates on wings will mix in leisure time or working time. In addition, there have always been educational provisions and religious elements inside prison walls.

Research into past lives aims to put together an overall timeline of a person's life, however sketchy; if a person led a life of crime and had several prison terms, then the more information that comes to light about the circumstances of the crimes, the more detailed the biography will be.

Prison returns and calendars will point towards a number of items in the social context, and often these relate to major events.

This context is where memoirs of prison life become so valuable. Right in the heart of all the social unrest of Britain in the Regency, with regular wars and much internal strife, Samuel Bamford, a radical, was accused of high treason and imprisoned awaiting trial. He came to know several of our prisons. His memoir, *Passages in the Life of a Radical*, shows that conditions in the prisons varied extremely. At one time, when remanded, he was put in one of the best:

My prison was now a pleasant one, compared with the cell I had quitted. To be sure, except my bed, everything around, beneath and above was of iron and stone ... The walls were very white; the floors were well stoned; my bed seemed very clean and there was a free current of air, as good as any gentleman in the neighbourhood breathed ...

One fascinating aspect of this is the notion of the *Weltanschauung* of a certain period. This German word refers to the general world picture of a given time; for instance, if we locate a prisoner in the last decades of the sixteenth century, under Elizabeth I, then it is not difficult to pick out the constituents of the *Weltanschauung* of the age: fear of invasion; the common incidence of treason; religious conflicts and the lack of control of public order. A look at the first half of the fourteenth century would present such massive world events as the Great Plague, wars in France, and starvation.

In archival material, prison documents will often link in the references to this larger picture, and sometimes a more universal slice of social history will directly relate to prison sentencing. A perfect instance of this would be the years of war with Revolutionary France and Napoleon (1790s–1815) when, as alternatives to prison, offenders might be drafted into the army.

The deeper understanding of prison lives is most easily accessed by the contemporary writers and documentation. Visitors to gaols, for instance, such as religious workers or philanthropic individuals, open up our knowledge of the lives inside. Then, in the Victorian period, when fact-gathering generated a flow of documentary publications, knowledge of the conditions in which our ancestors lived and worked becomes much more detailed. For the mid-Victorian period, for instance, Mayhew and Binny's *The Criminal Prisons of London* (1862) is a monumental work of statistics, explanation and documentation (see the Bibliography). Similarly, by the twentieth century, more professionals working in prisons wrote about their work, and much of this material filtered down into archive collections.

More direct information on prison lives will be found in the archives in the reports provided for local councils. For instance, in Lincoln, the returns for the prison in 1878 include this kind of expenditure-logging over a month:

Shaving and haircutting:	13/10
Tins repaired:	10/6
Straw:	16/6
Brown linsey for petticoats:	10/6
Stationery:	9/6
Warders' uniforms:	£19
Old rope for oakum	£14/10

The figures are in pounds, shillings and pence.

The last item refers to the work done by some prisoners, working on old ropes to make oakum for use on ships. As to linsey, this was 'linsey-wooly' fabric, coarse woven and strictly for the workers.

The prison life your ancestor led is indicated by the staff and by the expenditure. We know from bills and accounts registered what these were like. In the quarterly disbursements for one prison, we see that the principal staffing was one chaplain, a surgeon, the governor, the matron, a head-warder, two other warders, a cook and a gate porter. The food spending was mainly on bread, meat and vegetables, and per quarter these foodstuffs cost almost £46.

What about the conditions in the cells in Victorian prisons? We know that at Lincoln a Mr Cooke supplied 'furniture, bedding and stores in all parts of the prison' and that a Mrs Foster supplied the matron with 'articles of female clothing for those under her care'.

The returns of prison spending also point to the amounts actually used for the inmates' provisions. In 1878 we have this:

Ordered ... that the return of amount paid for maintenance of convicted prisoners for the half year ending September last amounting to £24.2.3 Now produced and signed be transmitted to the lords of the Treasury for payment.

The fundamental driving force behind the documents found in archives other than prison listings themselves was economy. In the years of the houses of correction, the institutions were factories, mills or workshops (or a combination of all these) which just happened to have convicts

The beginning of the legal process in Georgian Britain – a summons to court. (Author)

working the machines, and income generated would then fund the food, bedding and health treatments for other inmates who were not convicted criminals. This meant that the governor and his administration were always concerned with the accounts, running costs and figures relating to productivity.

Chapter 1

THE HISTORY OF PRISONS IN BRITAIN I

Crime and law before the assizes

Oliver Cyriax sums up the situation regarding prisons before the Tudor age:

> Historically, Britain had little need of prisons. If guilty, the normal sentence was death, and if innocent, the accused was released. The idea of sentencing miscreants to a fixed term of confinement did not evolve until more civilized times. (Penguin Encyclopaedia of Crime)

Locating a prisoner ancestor in the long period of time referred to as 'mediaeval' can be a formidable task. Records are widespread, piecemeal and often in forms and texts only accessible to learned scholars with arcane knowledge. But there are some approaches and methods, with relevant sources, which may help.

Before the widespread inspections made on prison visits by John Howard and others towards the end of the eighteenth century, our knowledge of particular prisons has come largely from local books and reports, often by antiquarians or visiting magistrates. Gaols after the Norman Conquest of 1066 and before the first assizes in 1166 were largely in castles and similar places. Local power (in the hands of the *Shire reeve* – later sheriff) imposed imprisonment in any place which could be secure.

Even after the first eyres (circuit courts), when the assize courts began to be established after the Assize of Clarendon in 1166, gaols were mainly created to keep prisoners secure until they could be tried. The assizes and eyres were the courts led by the sovereign's justices on the road. The eyres were not necessarily reliable or uniformly organised. In theory, there was an eyre every seven years, but this did not always happen.

Hearings at eyres were governed by commissions – royal assignments. The commissions were first of all an eyre, and then a gathering known as 'oyer et terminer' – to hear and conclude or decide. More directly concerned with deciding the fate of people awaiting their trials was the commission of gaol delivery (these are more fully explained below in this chapter). The general approach was to use these commissions to maintain justice and sort the guilty from the innocent. But prison played little part in this. There were exceptions, and in his wonderful journey into the mediaeval world, *The Time Traveller's Guide to Medieval England*, Ian Mortimer isolates one rare case:

> *Overall about a third of all the accused men are executed, the remainder being released. There are few other punishments. It is not unknown for a man to be given life imprisonment: Hugh le Bever of London ... is sent to prison for killing his wife, Alice, 'there to remain in penance until he should be dead'.*

Some of the earliest recorded gaols were in the last decades of the twelfth century. As early as 1165 there were gaols at Bedford, Aylesbury, Cambridge and Canterbury. Ipswich had a gaol in 1163. Not until houses of correction came into use, known also as bridewells, were prisons used as anything but pre-trial secure holding rooms.

Specific assizes through the mediaeval period dealt with certain defined areas of law, such as the *assize of novel disseisin*, formed in 1166 to take decisions regarding tenants who had been evicted. Such a person could take out a writ, and a sheriff could make a local jury to hear the plea. The assize went on until 1833.

When researchers come across ancestors who were on the wrong side of the law in mediaeval times, they mostly rely on publications by county record societies or, if they have Latin and very acute eyesight, they may study original documents from manorial courts and other specific courts. Fortunately, several record societies have supplied translations of court transactions. These include county record societies, and professional groups such as the Surtees Society (see Bibliography).

A clear example is in some publications of the Norfolk Record Society. The gaol at Norwich Castle was subject to a 'delivery' by the travelling justices (an assize) in October 1309. Thanks to scholars, historians may now use an index of names, and if their ancestor was Hugh le Bercher of Riston, then we have this:

Clackclose: *Hugh le Bercher of Riston was taken for stealing a certain cow worth 6s. From Joan Gerard. He comes and because the constable of* *the hundred of Clackclose, who made the indictment, is not here with the indictment of the aforesaid Hugh, he is returned to prison. The sheriff is ordered to distrain the aforesaid constable and have him here at the next delivery with the aforesaid indictment.*

The unfamiliar legal vocabulary is minimal, but needs explanation. The *indictment* is the statement of the charge. The sheriff will *distrain* his man: force him to attend. The *hundred* was a piece of land administered as a parcel of a larger area, and this meant something between a parish and a shire. There had been hundred courts since Saxon times. A writ is a written instruction to begin an action at law. Overall, the 'delivery' at the assize (emptying the gaol) was to fulfil these functions, and it was all in the hands of the justices working for the king. *Oyer and terminer* means to 'hear and determine' the offences committed in the county where the hearing occurs, and *gaol delivery* was the direction to decide on the fate of the prisoners who were imprisoned and waiting for the decision on their alleged crime. They could be 'delivered' (released), given a punishment, or, as in the case of Hugh le Bercher, sent back to his cell until there was an indictment. It was not possible to create the indictment on the spot, in new wording. The original one had to be there. The constable at Clackclose had let down the prisoner very badly. Hugh had to return to gaol and wait for the next assize. There were only three a year. That means he was subject to disease and infection within Norwich Castle prison and his life came to a standstill, putting him in the limbo of the prisoner.

There is also the question of the texts we must tackle from this period if we are to find the facts of the case. The documents will be very hard to read. Many of the court records will be in what was known as 'court hand'. This type of writing style, with distinctively long, sweeping letters, was used until as late as 1731 when the Proceedings in Courts of Justice Act decreed that documents should be written in 'a common legible hand and character'. The researcher needs to be aware of this.

Obviously, tracking down a prisoner from mediaeval times entails mastering these obstacles. It helps to bear in mind that the narrative of the whole court process and the outcomes of trials are needed to understand the imprisonment. For instance, in the mid-thirteenth century at Alton in Hampshire, there was a robbery. M.T. Clanchy summarises the trial results, taken from a plea roll:

Of the sixty-four persons charged either with being principals or accessories of the robbery, twenty-five were found guilty, twenty-five were acquitted, twelve were remanded in custody for lesser offences, and on two, no verdict was recorded. Of those found guilty, thirteen were outlawed in their absence, two escaped and abjured the realm, one was committed to the bishop as a clerk-convict and nine are presumed to have been hanged ...

What strikes the modern reader here is just how rare imprisonment was. Locking someone up was a burden: the prisoner would have to be fed and guarded. Even the one man held in this example was allotted a working role with the bishop.

Often, the minimal records showing punishments simply have the word 'gaole' and that could mean, in manorial times, any one of a variety of places. Yet, as well as accounts of crimes and trials, and of course the punishments meted out, there are other documents which highlight the names of those incarcerated. For example, there are crown pleas. The most relevant ones to the current subject are pleas from prisoners. Sometimes the plea is brief and precise, for example:

Presentment of Roger of Welhope. A sergeant of Thomas Corbet and his fellows took Richard of Norbury and imprisoned him at Cause; and Richard could not get free until he gave them 12 pence. So judgement on Roger.

In another case, a gang of men attacked William Piers of Brompton, who complained to the justices and said, 'they dragged him to prison and there they kept him for two days and two nights in shackles, wrongfully and against the peace ...' William managed to gather some friends to make pledges that he would prosecute.

Above and beyond all this, there was of course the Magna Carta of 1215, and although this was amended and edited later, its statements on imprisonment give the modern reader some hints as to how law and prison were seen at the time, in relation to individual rights. Here are the crucial statements:

In future no official shall put anyone to trial on his own testimony, without reliable witnesses produced for this purpose. No freeman shall be arrested or imprisoned or deprived of his freehold or outlawed or banished or in any way ruined, nor will we take our action against him, except by the lawful judgement of his equals and according to the law of the land.

No-one shall be arrested or imprisoned upon the appeal of a woman for the death of anyone except her husband.

Men who live outside the forest shall not henceforth come before the justices of our forest upon a general summons, unless they are impleaded or are sureties of any person under pledge to appear in connection upon forest offences. We will only appoint as justiciars, constables, sheriffs or bailiffs such as know the law ...

These extracts reflect the king's concerns now that there were assizes and travelling judges working on his behalf (the king being John, son of Edward II who reformed the law). John was most concerned with the forest laws and methods of impressing men to appear at assizes. There had obviously been outrageous flouting of humane and considerate behaviour on the part of the king's officers for many years, and this famous document, supposedly the foundation of much material eventually found in our common law, may be read as a stumbling attempt to recognise wrongs and mistakes in the system. But the above statements do help us make sense of the records from assizes.

For gaol delivery, sources at The National Archives under reference JUST 3 will lead the researcher to gaol delivery rolls covering the years 1271–1476. Linked to this are the gaol deliveries of the King's Bench at KB 27. As The National Archives site explains, the material is arranged in chronological order linked to groups of counties.

What you will find in these rolls comprises pleadings, commissions, and, in some cases, prison calendars. The bundles will also contain writs

A table of the Georgian assize circuits. (Gentleman's Magazine, 1806)

and pardons, and these are not an easy read. An important point to note is explained on The National Archives site:

> *During the fifteenth century the circuit clerks ceased to compile gaol delivery rolls or return gaol delivery files to the Exchequer, and so these records virtually cease for nearly a century, until 1559.*

To use and understand these documents, some explanation of a *writ* is needed. A writ is a written directive in which an action is commanded to be done. At first, these would be the documents sent to a defendant summoning the person to appear. There are also judicial writs, which are issued by a court. One of the most common writs in criminal records is the *'certiorari'*, which ordered process to be changed from an inferior court to a superior one. This was abolished in 1938.

The inferior courts are the smaller, regional and sectional courts, and originally they were subject to regulation and supervision by the Court of King's or Queen's Bench (superior).

Criminals in other early records

While not directly concerned with prison, early sources do give opportunities for researchers to see and understand criminal deviance at times long before the official penal records.

A survey of early records and sources will be invaluable here. Basically, everything we might call a source for prisons and prisoners before the establishment of the Home Office in 1782 presents linguistic and formal difficulties. But it is worthwhile to attempt to go further back in time, before the late Georgian emergence of prison records *per se*.

First, there are pipe rolls, which have that name because they were stored in rolls around a pipe or a rod. Their purpose was to monitor returns of accounts from property, along with expenses incurred by Crown officers, and they extend from 1131 to 1831. Although they do not pertain to prison as such, they do include offences.

An exceptional instance is an account of a transgressor, Alexander of Torksey, in the king's forest in 1201. The case stood out because the king was there at the time. This happened at Stow in Lincolnshire. The offender escaped prison but was fined. Nigel Burn, who has written about the case, quotes the pipe roll: 'Alexander of Torksey, a clerk, owes 50 marks and a palfrey and two greyhounds to be quit of the offence of hunting for which he was taken in Stow Park ...'

The interest here lies in the fact that, on very many occasions, the crown and the legal professionals were much keener to take money and valuable goods from a criminal than to clap him in gaol.

The principles behind this go back a very long way. In Bede's classic work, *A History of the English Church and People* (written in 731 AD), he writes:

> *The punishment must depend on the circumstances of the offender. For some commit theft even though they have means of subsistence, and others out of poverty. Some, therefore, should be punished by fines, others by beating; some severely and others more leniently. But when the punishment is severe, let it be administered in charity ...*

In addition, there are manorial records, and these are in the form of Baron Courts and Court Leets. Again, though not concerned with gaols and prisoners, they do include accounts of criminality. The National Archives include these. There are also church courts, and although most of the punishments in these were fines, there was also reference to imprisonment because, naturally, offences which would bring custodial sentences would usually progress from initial hearings through to major courts. In the 1784 Countess of Strathmore case, for instance, Stoney Bowes, husband of Mary, Countess of Strathmore, was imprisoned for kidnap after a long and eventful series of hearings.

Varieties of gaols

William Piers was most likely thrown into a dungeon. Any dark cell could meet that definition, but what about an oubliette? Dungeons and oubliettes were lower-level enclosed cells underground beneath large buildings such as a castles. The oubliette, which comes from the French *oublier* 'to forget', was a bottle-neck dungeon.

We need to add another dimension to the gaols of the mediaeval period: the religious one. Andrew McCall, a specialist on crime in this early period, explains in his book *The Medieval Underworld* that from the thirteenth century prison as a punishment was more in favour, but he adds:

> *In the monastic Rule of St. Benedict Roman Law's distaste for imprisonment seems to have prevailed ... but the advantages to the Church of a punishment which gave the offender time to reflect on his sins and repent soon made themselves obvious ...*

A spell in such a monastic gaol was not a welcome prospect for an offender, especially a poor one. Gaolers were always open to bribery, and there was little regulation, control and supervision.

THE
Bloody Assizes:
Or, A Compleat
HISTORY
OF THE
LIFE
OF
George Lord Jefferies,
FROM

His Birth to this Present Time.

WHEREIN,

Among other things, is given a true Account of his unheard of Cruelties, and Barbarous Proceedings, in his whole **Western Circuit**.

COMPREHENDING

The whole Proceedings; Arraignment, Tryals, and Condemnation of all those who Suffer'd in the *West* of *England*, in the Year 1685. With their undaunted Courage at the Barr, their Behaviour in Prison, their Cruel Whippings afterwards, and the remarkable Circumstances that attended their Executions.

To which is added Major *HOLMES's* Excellent Speech, with the Dying Speeches and Prayers of many other Eminent Protestants.

None of which were ever before Publish'd.

Faithfully Collected by several West-Countrey Gentlemen, who were both Eye and Ear-Witnesses to all the matter of Fact.

WITH ALLOWANCE.

LONDON, Printed for **J. Dunton** at the *Black Raven* in the *Poultrey*, over against the *Compter*, and sold by R. *Janeway* in *Queens-Head-Alley* in *Pater-noster-row*. 1680.

An example of early true crime, based on the worst elements of assize trials. (Author)

The monasteries and abbeys do provide sources for prisoner information, as they often include journals and registers which deal with all local matters. At the Abbey of Peterborough, for instance, the register has information about the gaol delivery in 1400:

> *the prison of John Coraunt, and their fellow justices, is entered in the abbey register. The prisoners included four who were* notorii latrones *[notable robbers], nine horse stealers, one sheep stealer ... one utterer of forged money, nine suspected of robbery ... There were twenty-seven prisoners of whom several were acquitted and five hung.*

Of special interest here is that John Coraunt (a private citizen) had his own gaol.

The Assizes

The story of the assize courts is a reflection of how the criminal law gradually developed into a system which would have parity across the land. The courts represent the boldest step by which central legal power began to cover the king's domains, using local and national elements together. In each shire, the sheriff, who had been there since very early times, gathered the jury and the other machinery of law, ready for the visit of the assize judges, because that is what assizes were – regular visiting courts – giving the assize towns distinguished visitors and a high level of ritual and importance for a few days each year.

Originally the law courts followed the king around the country, and his own court was the *Curia Regis*. Then in Magna Carta (1215) came this sentence: 'Common pleas shall not follow our Court but shall be held in some certain place'. The result was that Westminster was made that 'place', but then the notion of having the top judges moving around to deal with criminal and civil cases became a workable option, with economic and logistical benefits, as persons accused would be retained and then tried mostly in their own counties or provinces.

Since early mediaeval times, there had been assizes – literally 'sittings together' – to try causes and to gather officials in the English regions to compile enquiries and inventories into local possessions and actions. The assize courts came when travelling justices went out into the counties to try cases: the Assize of Clarendon in 1166 and the Council of Northampton in 1196 decreed that the country should be split into six areas in which the judges of the High Court would sit. These became known as circuits.

In Edward I's reign an act was passed to create court hearings in the local place of jury trial, before a summons for the jury to go to Westminster. The people involved were to come to London unless the trial had happened before: in Latin *nisi prius* (unless before). What developed over the centuries was that serious offences, crimes needing an *indictment*, had to be tried before a jury. The less serious offences, summary ones, could be tried by a magistrate. In addition to that, the terms *felony* and *misdemeanour* existed until they were abolished in 1967: a felony was a crime in which guilt would mean a forfeiture of possessions and land, so the offender's children would lose their inheritance. A misdemeanour was a less serious crime.

The reign of Henry II is crucially important in the establishment of assizes. His recent biographer, Claudia Gold, explains:

Henry called several assizes (meetings between himself and his barons which issued binding decrees) between 1166 and 1184. They numbered the Assize of Clarendon of 1166, which dealt with criminal law; the assize of Northampton of 1176, which increased the powers of Henry's justices; and the assize of the forest of 1184 which ensured that forests were brought within the law.

The justices of assizes had a number of powers. First, they had a commission of *oyer and terminer* (to listen and to act) on serious cases such as treason, murder, and any crime which was labelled a felony. They also had to try all people who had been charged and who had been languishing in gaol since their arrest, and they tried cases *nisi prius*.

The assizes became established as the Home, Midland, Norfolk, Oxford, Eastern, Western and Northern circuits, and the records for these run from 1558 to either 1864 or 1876 when assizes were reorganised, or to 1971, when the assizes were abolished and crown courts created (though the circuits continue, of course). From the beginning, the assize circuits covered all counties except Cheshire, Durham, Lancashire and Middlesex, the first three being referred to as the Palatinate Courts. In 1876, some courts moved from one circuit to another.

Records for these courts began to be more systematically kept after 1559. There are gaps, such as the years 1482–1559, in listings – calendars of assizes. Most records before 1733 are in Latin.

For early records, materials are in TNA at JUST 1–JUST 4 and there are indictments for these earlier times in the King's Bench records at KB9, and some letters from assize judges at SP1. Then, from 1559, if the researcher knows the name of the prisoner and where the trial took place, the next step is to find the assize records at the County Record Office. At TNA there are sheriff's assize vouchers, but only for 1714–1832, so if there are no assize records locally for those years, then the vouchers will help. They are concerned with costs incurred for moving, watching and feeding prisoners. There is also a series of Calendars of State Prisoners online at https://www.british-history.ac.uk. The Domestic series includes criminal cases.

The stages of enquiry are:

- First, check the probable dates and place of the offence.
- Look in *The Times Digital Archive* for a court report, searching with the criminal's name or the assize location. These are under the 'assizes' and crown court' terms.
- At the record office where the assizes records are held, look at the calendar of prisoners.
- Search for any other documents relating to the trial.

Case study: York Castle

A look at the York Castle prison as it was in the Middle Ages gives a clear impression of what a prison was like in the time before the first bridewells. As a fortress, its history stretches back to just after the Norman Conquest of 1066. Development and rebuilding was done over the succeeding centuries, and by the eighteenth century it included a prison.

Listings in a catalogue which was reproduced in a volume of the Yorkshire Archaeological Society give a detailed log of 'victims of the law executed at or from York Castle for political or criminal offences'. However, the catalogue is far from comprehensive and the editor points out that 'the records at the castle have not been comprehensively kept'. Nevertheless, we have names of everyday villains such as 'Edward Hewison ... a criminal, guilty of rape' in 1379. This is alongside the political prisoners, from the Duke of York down to Sir William Hill in 1460 and 1463 respectively.

The prison itself has had its scholarly historians: William Knipe in 1867 and T.P. Cooper, whose work was published in 1911. Knipe provided only a few names from the pre-Tudor period, once again showing the difficulty of locating earlier prisoners. The people he does include have become visible because of riot, disorder and factional revolt. So, for instance, 'John Chambers and others' are mentioned in his entry for 27 November 1488. Knipe explains:

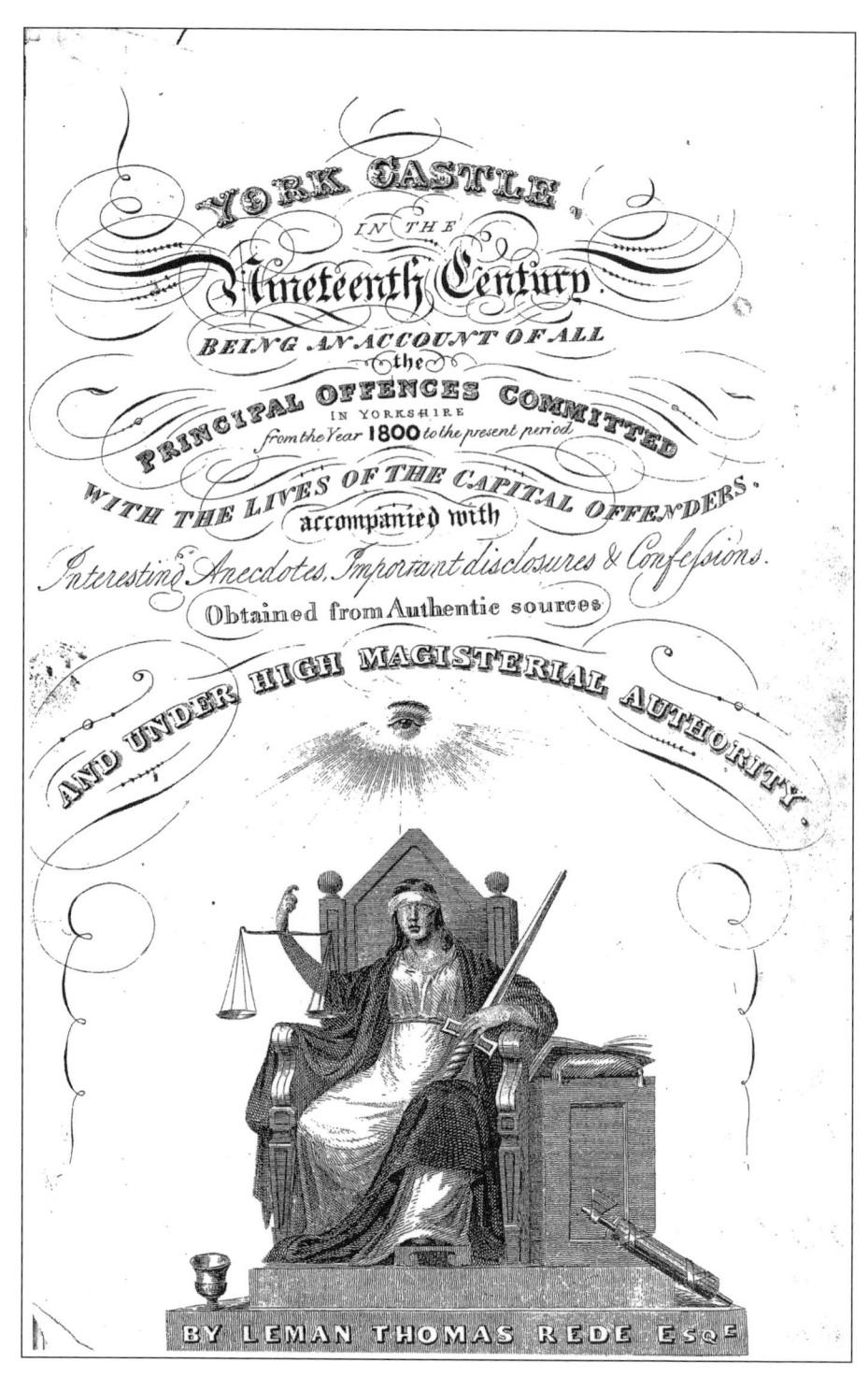

Frontispiece from Leman Rede's collection of prisoner biographies in 1829. (Author)

During this year a tax of a tenth of a penny was laid on men's goods and lands to aid the Duke of Bretagne against the French king, which caused an insurrection amongst the people of the north.

Cooper's book gives more information on the origins of the prison. He notes that the first mention of the gaol within the castle is in 1205. His comments on the gaolers explain the awful situation of the prisoners there:

We in our time, can hardly realize the callousness practised by these farming gaolers. They, free from government control, cruelly preyed upon their prisoners, who ... had to pay a fee on entering gaol and another before the gaolers would set them free. Many were kept in prison after their terms of sentence had expired, because they were penniless and unable to fee or bribe their keepers for release.

The records are patchy, but at least Cooper provides a listing of gaolers, prison governors and custodians, and these cover the years 1280–1484 as well as the Reformation period and beyond.

If explanations are needed of the conditions in these early times –the years of those dungeons and oubliettes – then Cooper provides some insights, including the only available sources for the mediaeval years. He points out that it is in the pipe rolls from the reign of King John that records of prisoners are found. Yet, more often than not, the information given is of money spent and repairs rather than lists of inmates.

Surely the most powerful and informative notion we have of mediaeval prisoners is not on vellum, but on glass. In a 'six works of mercy' window at All Saints' Church in the city there is a panel showing a group of prisoners, shackled with collars and chains, their legs held in the clamp as in the village stocks we see in later remains.

Some few sources give names of prisoners, and in these the reader learns something of the kinds of offences which led to incarceration. For instance, as Cooper notes:

The sheriff was ordered by Edward I on October 26th [1291] to deliver Richard le Keu, imprisoned for a trespass in the King's Fishpond of Fosse, wherewith he is charged, in bail to malpernors [those who provide surety that the prisoner will appear in court] *who shall undertake To have him before the justices whom the King shall appoint to hear and determine this trespass.*

On the whole, the prison at York within the castle, before the new prison built in the Georgian period, illustrates the features of prisons in the mediaeval years before the first steps towards regulation and before local government involvement. These features could be summed up as ad hoc, cruel and repressive and punitive.

The records of prisoners are only to be found in documents of manorial courts and other materials relating to administration of land and to assize trials.

There is no doubt that the lot of the mediaeval prisoner was miserable in the extreme. The evidence is there in the Rolls of the courts; and of an early assize at Ludinglond, in the reign of Henry III, there is this record:

Assizes held at Ludinglond. The jury present that William le Sauvage took two men, aliens, and one woman, and imprisoned them at Thorlestan, and detained them in prison until one of them died in prison, and the other lost one foot, and the woman lost either foot by putrefaction. Afterwards he took them to the court of the Lord the King at Ludinglond to try them by the same court. And when the court saw them, it was loth to try them, because they were not attached for any robbery or misdeed for which they could suffer judgement. And so they were permitted to depart.

Chapter 2

THE HISTORY OF PRISONS IN BRITAIN II

The first Bridewell and Tudor imprisonment

In 1598, John Stow wrote his *Survey of London*, in which he gives an account of how what was once a home for kings back in the mediaeval period became a prison. The place in question was Bridewell, and that word became a generalised term for houses of correction, as they became known later. Stow explains:

> *But you now shall hear how this house became a house of correction. In the year 1553, the 7th of King Edward VI., the 10th of April, Sir George Baron, being mayor of this city, was sent for to the court at Whitehall, and … the king gave unto him for the commonalty and citizens, to be a workhouse for the poor and idle persons of the city …*

In 1555 Bridewell began its life as a gaol. When John Howard visited in the 1770s, he made plenty of positive remarks about the way it was run. He found it to be a fairly healthy establishment, saying, for instance, 'The women's rooms are large, and have opposite windows for fresh air. Their ward, as well as the men's has water: and there is a hand-ventilator on the outside'.

Bridewell became a model for the houses of correction, a mix of factories, homes for debtors and vagrants, and holding buildings for both political and criminal prisoners. When humanely run, they did essential work reclaiming those people who otherwise would have drifted into decline and death. Unfortunately, it took a long time for regulation by local justices to be fully effective.

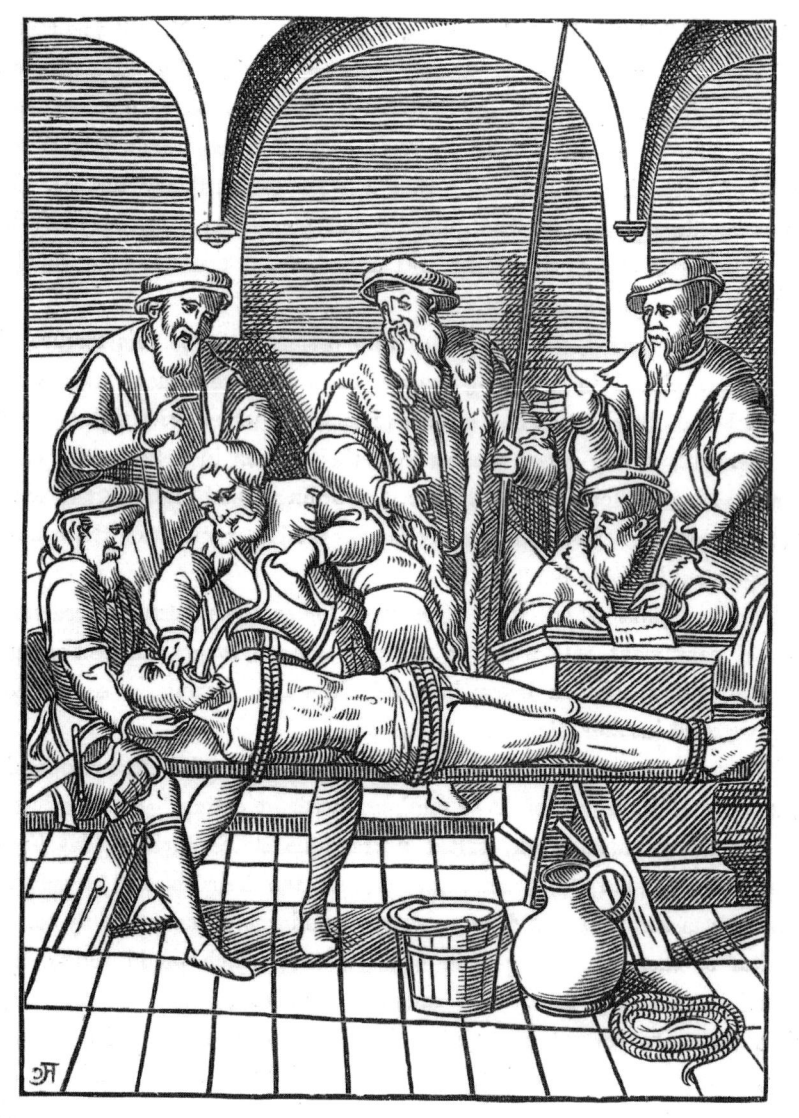

Fig. 341.—The Water Torture.—Fac-simile of a Woodcut in J. Damhoudère's "Praxis Rerum Criminalium:" in 4to, Antwerp, 1556.

An illustration from Fox's Book of Martyrs *showing the treatment of some prisoners in Tudor jails. (Author)*

Local systems and houses of correction

British prisons, from Tudor times through to the mid-nineteenth century, worked using local systems. This carried right through from finance to administration and supervision. In the early nineteenth century, the *Gentleman's Magazine* had built on Howard's work by having a travelling reporter visit and write about a selection of local gaols. This was all done in a spirit of documentary, but also with the Enlightenment values of humanitarian care and regulation in mind.

In the early phase of such gaols, the concerns of the parish were very much involved, as the quarter sessions and the Bench had to be concerned with everything from nuisances on the highway to military deserters and bastardy. Often crimes were committed by people who were from another parish, and so poor law came into the interaction as well.

Those same justices on the bench also had to spend their time visiting their prison and meeting to discuss and decide any expenditure. Their reports give a fascinating picture of a specific gaol – perhaps your ancestor's. A typical report notes physical conditions, health care and working arrangements. Such practical affairs as heating were in the hands of technical specialists, such as Haden.

Even a century after the Gaol Acts brought about by Sir Robert Peel in the 1820s, reporters were still very much concerned with every detail of the living conditions:

The gate house is small and very short and the inner gate of very light construction. On the right is the Gate Office, with sleeping-in room over, on the left a waiting room and a store for books ...

The records of many of the fleeting, transitory guests of His Majesty back in Regency times are often no more than a sentence written by the keeper. These are some examples from a keeper's journal from the years 1833–1838 at Huntingdon County Gaol:

13 October 1833: Locked up Mary Austen for disorderly conduct in the chapel this morning.

20 October: Locked up Edward Raynor for conversing with other prisoners when confined in their cells.

9 November: Locked up Edward Arthur for making a loud noise in his cell after he had been confined therein for the night.

Solitary confinement was central to the running of the gaols. The germ of this punishment lies in the gradual switch from a constant application of physical punishment to one of deprivation. By the 1820s the notion lay behind the latest concepts of rehabilitation, but in the local gaols which Howard saw, we have a good idea of how the refractory cells were used. The gaol registers at Maidstone show a typical range of cases. J. Savage was confined to a dark cell for three days 'persuant to the order of the visiting magistrate', and 'Confined to dark cell for three days, Mary Burrell, on the report from the matron that she had used improper language respecting the chaplain and for riotous conduct'. At the same gaol in 1821, William Constable and George Merchant were confined in dark cells, Constable for assaulting and beating James Styles, Merchant for singing in his sleeping cell.

A survey of some instances of the application of solitary confinement in the years between 1790 and 1830 shows that it was a controversial topic, but it was generally accepted as the most severe punishment except for the lash. Some of the sentences given in court specified solitary rather than the usual gaol regime, as in the case of John Webb in 1828, who was in court for stealing three pewter pots from a pub in St James's. A female servant testified against him, and Webb, from the dock, took off a nailed shoe and violently threw it at her, striking her on the arm. The judge said that such an action deserved 'the heaviest penalty of the law' and that meant imprisonment in Newgate for six months, the whole time to be spent in solitary, to be followed by seven years of transportation.

Clearly, solitary confinement, though a regular short-term punishment in local gaols, was a special case in the general actions taken in sentencing. In 1816, William Price was sentenced at the West Sussex quarter sessions to six months' solitary confinement on bread and water for stealing a leaden weight. It was also seen as an essential punishment for young criminals, with the attitude that it would deter them from further transgression. In 1831 at the Thames Police Court, an eleven-year-old girl called Isabella Brown was charged with stealing property from her employer in Commercial Road. The girl's mother begged the magistrates to do something to 'check the girl's propensity for pilfering', and the sentence was fourteen days in the house of correction to be in solitary confinement.

There were some voices of dissent and some were troubled by the idea of the 'dark cell'. In 1827 at the Surrey Asylum for the reformation of Discharged Prisoners there was a committee meeting at which this interchange took place:

> *an objection was placed by Mr Hedger to having persons placed in solitary confinement, conceiving the punishment too great. This mode of dealing with delinquents was stated to be very efficacious, and those who entered the Society had the rules read to them before they were admitted ... The Honorary secretary said that at the Hoxton Institution, solitary confinement for offenders had done a great deal of good. It was at length*

A picture from a Victorian religious work. (Earnest Lives 1884)

agreed to, instead of using the words 'solitary confinement', 'separated from other inmates' should be substituted.

This classic example of euphemism and double-think would have been ridiculous to the area of society in which solitary confinement was used most barbarically: in the army and navy, although this was banned in the 1840s. In all the annals of corporal punishment in British imprisonment, arguably the most repulsive and savage use of solitary confinement was that described by an officer of the Royal Marines in a letter to the press in 1832. It concerns a private in the Royal North Lincolnshire Militia who, in 1804, struck at his sergeant-major with the butt-end of his musket. At a court martial he was sentenced to 1,000 lashes and three months in solitary confinement in the black hole of the main guardhouse. He was given the first 500 lashes and drummed out of the regiment.

The reformers, when they began to emerge on the scene, had ample material to work on when it came to arguing for humanitarian treatment. Some events in prison history would have been enough to persuade authorities that reform was needed. On one occasion, typhus was brought by prisoners into a court and virtually everyone present died of the infection.

John Howard

John Howard, arguably the most famous name in the history of prison reform, produced his great work, *The State of the Prisons*, in 1777. Over seventeen years he surveyed every English prison, and he also ventured into Europe with the same humanitarian purpose. On the topic of gaol fever he was direct and shocking, pointing out that from his own observations in the years between 1773 and 1775, he was fully convinced that 'many more prisoners were destroyed by it than were put to death by all the public executions in the kingdom'. He noted that there was on record an assize held at Oxford in 1577 in which all who were present died within 48 hours. At Taunton in 1730 'some prisoners who were brought there from Ilchester gaol infected the court and Lord Chief Baron Pengelly, Sir James Sheppard, John Piggot, sheriff and some hundreds besides died of the gaol distemper …'.

A typical example of Howard's reporting on health is this from Cambridge:

> *In the spring, seventeen women were confined in the daytime and some of them at night in this room, which has no fire-place or sewer. This made it extremely offensive, and occasioned a fever or sickness among them which alarmed the Vice-Chancellor who ordered all of them to be discharged. Two or three died within two days …*

Some of the stories involving gaol fever from the Georgian years are heart-rending in the extreme. A man called Burt, for example, was convicted of forgery in 1790. He refused a pardon when offered one and was determined to hang because, he said, of a 'disappointment in love'. But he then won the lady over, and she came to see him in gaol, where she caught the fever and died. His life of adventure continued, because he was transported to Sydney, but while on board ship he wrote to a barrister he knew in Lincoln's Inn to inform him of a conspiracy being hatched on the ship. He was taken into the captain's cabin for protection. In Australia he managed to start life again.

Howard had his own recommendations for improvement. He believed that washing and fresh air were essential, and that a small stream running near the courtyard pump would help. He recalled that he had known of a prisoner supposed dead from the fever who was about to be buried and was being washed down with cold water, who then recovered, much to the shock and trauma of the layers-out.

Later writers provided commentaries on the lamentable condition of the prisons, and most had been influenced by Howard. For instance, if anyone studying the history of British prisons in the Georgian period needed any persuading that the system was cruel and inhuman, he or she need only read this entry from the journal of Charles Greville:

> *I went on Friday to the Old Bailey to hear the trials, particularly that of the women for the murder of the apprentices; the mother was found guilty and will be hanged today ... These wretched beings were described to be in the lowest state of moral and physical degradation, with scarcely rags to cover them, food barely sufficient to keep them alive, and working eighteen or nineteen hours a day, without being permitted any relaxation ...*

The prisoners, a mother and daughter named Hibner, were in a low state, but Greville points to the horrendous social conditions of the poor victims of the women. In other words, the state of the prisons was bad, but there were other aspects of society which showed the terrible extremes of poverty that existed in the metropolis. In this atmosphere, the press for reform went forward, leading to the Gaol Acts under Robert Peel.

If you find out that your ancestor was imprisoned in the last decades of the eighteenth century, then reading Howard's monumental book, *The State of the Prisons* will give you a reasonable idea of the conditions of the gaol the person was held in. These were local prisons, run by a group of justices, who employed a gaoler and any other staff they could afford. But the system relied on 'garnish' – money given to the gaoler for food and drink.

Howard, as well as giving details of conditions, fees and staffing at all the London gaols, went out into the shires. A typical report is in this extract from his feelings regarding the Essex county gaol at Chelmsford:

The old prison was close, and frequently infected with the gaol-distemper [typhus]. Inquiring in October 1775 for the head-turnkey, I was told he died of it.

In the tap-room there hung a paper on which, among other things, was written: 'Prisoners to pay garnish or run the gauntlet'.

It gave me pain to be informed in 1775, that there had been no divine service for above a year past, except to condemned criminals .... The prison was finished and occupied at the time of my visit in 1779.

Howard was generally pleased with Chelmsford, but he criticised the overcrowding. However, there was work going on, and he noted, 'Many were weaving garters'.

Howard (1726–1790) not only toured the British prisons, but also European ones, and it was in Russia, at Kherson, that he died. His name lives on in the Howard League for Penal Reform today.

Case study: Beverley house of correction

Here is a gaol with a rare distinction: it was the first place where Dick Turpin was held.

The life of this prison in Beverley, as it was in its nineteenth-century form, and being an important prison for the East Riding of Yorkshire, covers the years 1810 to 1878, reflecting the national trend from local gaol to the newer variety in line with the new legislation of 1877. There had been a much earlier one, which was operating in 1584, run by the local justices and by the corporation. This moved to another location in 1611, using part of Beverley Guildhall.

During the seventeenth century expansions in building were done, until in 1710 it became a much more industry-oriented place. Accommodation for lunatic residents came in 1742 and in 1785 there was more room for vagrants and mentally ill people. When it became the borough prison in 1810, it had workshops and by 1835 it had 126 cells. In the mid-Victorian years its population averaged around seventy.

A plan of 1853 shows separate exercise yards for male and female inmates, a central governor's house, kitchens, a turnkeys' room, and the court house and grand jury room, as the court area was incorporated into the house.

12

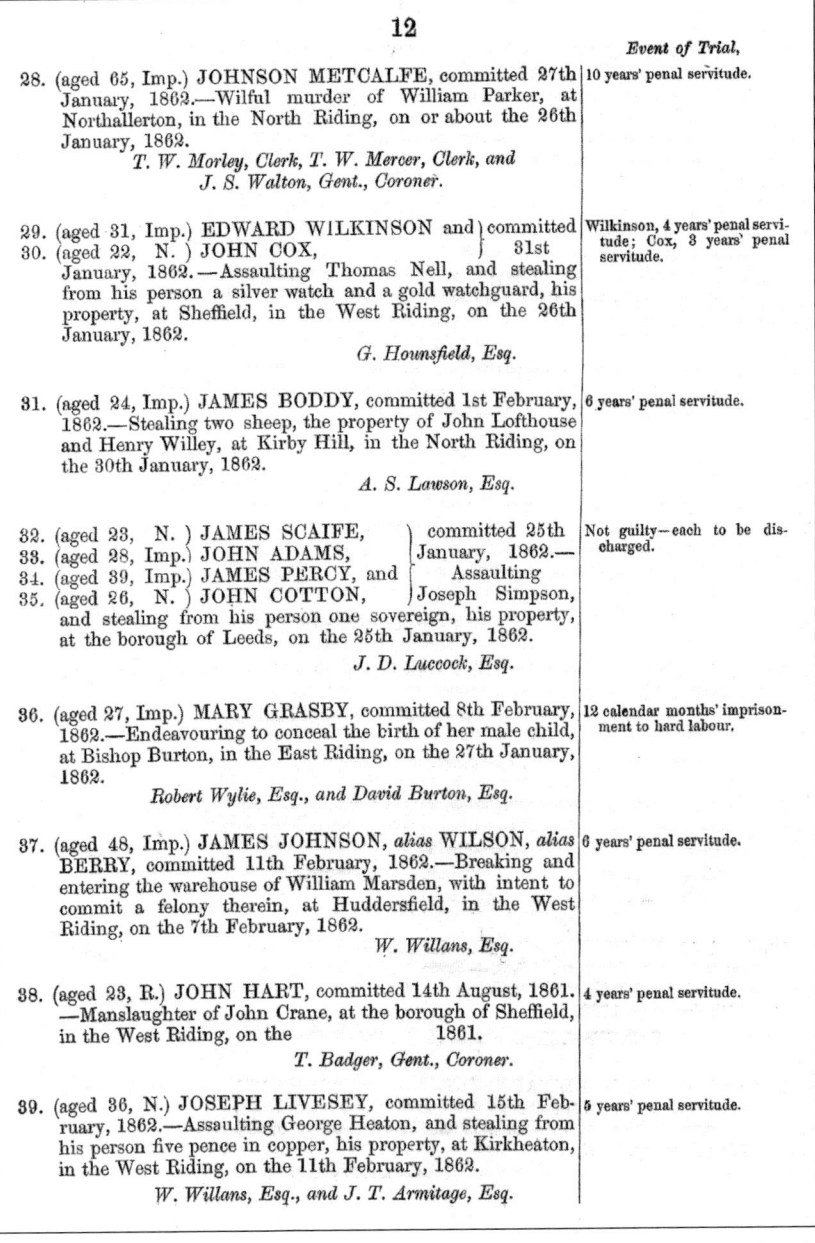

	Event of Trial.
28. (aged 65, Imp.) JOHNSON METCALFE, committed 27th January, 1862.—Wilful murder of William Parker, at Northallerton, in the North Riding, on or about the 26th January, 1862. *T. W. Morley, Clerk, T. W. Mercer, Clerk, and J. S. Walton, Gent., Coroner.*	10 years' penal servitude.
29. (aged 31, Imp.) EDWARD WILKINSON and } committed 30. (aged 22, N.) JOHN COX, } 31st January, 1862.—Assaulting Thomas Nell, and stealing from his person a silver watch and a gold watchguard, his property, at Sheffield, in the West Riding, on the 26th January, 1862. *G. Hounsfield, Esq.*	Wilkinson, 4 years' penal servitude; Cox, 3 years' penal servitude.
31. (aged 24, Imp.) JAMES BODDY, committed 1st February, 1862.—Stealing two sheep, the property of John Lofthouse and Henry Willey, at Kirby Hill, in the North Riding, on the 30th January, 1862. *A. S. Lawson, Esq.*	6 years' penal servitude.
32. (aged 23, N.) JAMES SCAIFE,) committed 25th 33. (aged 28, Imp.) JOHN ADAMS, } January, 1862.— 34. (aged 39, Imp.) JAMES PERCY, and } Assaulting 35. (aged 26, N.) JOHN COTTON,) Joseph Simpson, and stealing from his person one sovereign, his property, at the borough of Leeds, on the 25th January, 1862. *J. D. Luccock, Esq.*	Not guilty—each to be discharged.
36. (aged 27, Imp.) MARY GRASBY, committed 8th February, 1862.—Endeavouring to conceal the birth of her male child, at Bishop Burton, in the East Riding, on the 27th January, 1862. *Robert Wylie, Esq., and David Burton, Esq.*	12 calendar months' imprisonment to hard labour.
37. (aged 48, Imp.) JAMES JOHNSON, *alias* WILSON, *alias* BERRY, committed 11th February, 1862.—Breaking and entering the warehouse of William Marsden, with intent to commit a felony therein, at Huddersfield, in the West Riding, on the 7th February, 1862. *W. Willans, Esq.*	6 years' penal servitude.
38. (aged 23, R.) JOHN HART, committed 14th August, 1861.—Manslaughter of John Crane, at the borough of Sheffield, in the West Riding, on the 1861. *T. Badger, Gent., Coroner.*	4 years' penal servitude.
39. (aged 36, N.) JOSEPH LIVESEY, committed 15th February, 1862.—Assaulting George Heaton, and stealing from his person five pence in copper, his property, at Kirkheaton, in the West Riding, on the 11th February, 1862. *W. Willans, Esq., and J. T. Armitage, Esq.*	5 years' penal servitude.

Returns from a trial at the East Riding Spring Assize for 1862. (East Riding Archives)

The local justices and governor, along with the staff, managed the prison in the early phase, before the Gaol Acts of the 1820s began the slow process of reform and reorganisation. The 1823 Act began a series of reforms which reduced the number of capital offences; Acts in 1823 and

1824 brought about a number of rules and regulations for the running of gaols, and introduced the system of visiting justices for inspection purposes. In 1835 Home Office inspectors began to be involved in prison visits.

A typical communication from the Home Office to the Beverley house shows how meticulous the planning for changes was:

> *Lord John Russell desires me to acquaint you, for the information of the magistrates, that the Gaols Acts are about to be submitted to a Select Committee of the House of Commons and will probably undergo some revision ...*

The new general code for management was still being prepared in 1825.

What followed, into the mid-Victorian period, was a series of reports and regulations, mostly made by the visiting justices. In 1861, for instance, they noted 'sanitary condition of prison is very satisfactory' and 'The number of the ill during the year have been very few in number, and almost all were in a state of disease when admitted ...'

Rules were constantly amended and revised. In 1866 one report said, 'I would recommend that the table of hard labour be annexed to the rules'. More and more tabular information was gathered and archived as time went on, and there is more logging of staff and duties. In the 1850s, for instance, the 'Return of the establishment of officers' listed: Gaoler, matron, turnkey, chaplain, surgeon, watchman, schoolmaster, clerk, miller.

As we have today, there was very detailed job description material, as in this extract from the surgeon's duties:

> *The surgeon should attend the prison twice in every week and shall visit the sick himself and in case of his own sickness or unavoidable absence he shall depute some other practising surgeon of Beverley ...*

Conditions were impressively maintained as healthy and clean. Notes given in reports stipulate the measures taken to keep a smoothly-running gaol: 'The prison shall be limewashed once a year at least' is a typical order. As for discipline, keeping silence in the gaol was foremost, and those breaking that basic rule could be placed in solitary confinement or 'deprived of supper'.

Chapter 3

STAFF AND THE REGIME

Understanding the workers inside

Whatever the word stuck onto the prison officer, the fact is that the job is, and has always been, extremely demanding in all kinds of ways: the officer has to cope with discipline problems, develop working relationships (purely professional) with individuals; deal with a range of prison orders; liaise with the white-collar management (in a separate building to the prison usually) and also handle shift-work and such tiring, selfless tasks as 'bed-watch' when the officer has to make constant, round-the-clock observation of a prisoner at suicide risk.

In the local gaols before the 1877 Act which began the national regulation of prisons, the staff would be a mix of family members,

A photo showing the staff at Northallerton when it was developed into a prison rather than a house of correction. (Ripon Police Museum)

local part-timers, amateur medics and ex-military types. By the 1920s, there were more moves to change and improve the turnkey's lot. The first training initiatives were established, and over the last fifty years, in particular after a stormy period of prison violence in the 1960s, there has been more recognition of the necessity of giving support and respect to the people who work in this tough job.

In the mid-Victorian years our most remarkable insights into prison staff come from documentary narratives, such as the massive survey of London prisons undertaken by Henry Mayhew and John Binny in the 1850s, and from a strange work called *Female Life in Prison*, purporting to be written by 'a prison matron', but which was the work of F.W. Robinson. He summarised the women workers in this way:

> *In charge of the female compartment are assistant matrons on probation, assistant matrons, latterly a chief matron – on whom the practical running of the prison really devolves, but to whom credit is rarely given – a lady superintendent, a deputy governor and a governor.*

Basically there was a hierarchy of staff above the standard status of 'wardress', and we know only limited details of their daily work. Much may be inferred, though, and we may be sure that it was hard, demanding work.

Mayhew and Binny do give some enlightening statistics however. In their account of Brixton female prison, they supply a full list of staff as it was in 1856. The hierarchy was: principal officers and clerks, officers in the manufacturing and labour department, and subordinate officers and servants.

In the first group, of fourteen positions, seven were women, being the four members of the school staff, a scripture reader and two superintendents. In the second group, numbering just six staff, two were women, being the work mistress and the cutter. Finally, in the third group, there was a total of forty-seven staff, and of these, only seven were male: the carpenter, plumber, labourer, messenger, watchman, gatekeeper and baker. The predominantly female staff consisted of nineteen assistant matrons, thirteen matrons and three principal matrons. We may see from this that, in most cases, references to 'wardresses' meant matrons. Interestingly, the male equivalent terminology was 'warder' or even 'turnkey'.

Mayhew and Binny provide engraving illustrations of some female staff at that time. The principal matron wore a full-length, full dress, a collared cape, a blouse and a bonnet. As with most prison supervision,

Return showing some of the cost of running a Victorian prison. (East Riding Archives)

the work was tedious in the extreme for the matrons. One typical illustration in *Criminal Prisons of London* shows lines of women convicts at work on the landings, and three levels, sewing or picking oakum, while five matrons look on, standing throughout the shift.

One source that opens up prison workers' lives very powerfully is the state enquiry. In Parliamentary papers, staff are named and questioned regarding their daily work, and of course, their tasks and responsibilities come through very clearly in these texts.

Purposeful activity

This phrase sums up the nature (and certainly the wishful thinking) of those who manage prisons. Still, today, the aim of having every inmate busy outside his or her cell is 'devoutly to be wished', yet often in practice it does not happen. There are always too many imponderables in a prison regime; some people will be ill, others will have interviews or visits, still others might be undergoing court appearances or even time in solitary. The notion of having every inmate busy at work or study is and always has been an aspiration rather than an achievement.

Before the 1877 reorganisation of the British prison service, this aim was easier to achieve, however. Inmates were mostly poor and had no funds for extra-estate links and communications; the stress was on basic schooling, physical labour and time in prayer and self-reflection.

Even before the advent of extensive and meticulous record-keeping in the later reformed prison estate, there was a desperate need to log activity, work and play, and of course, religious instruction. In the bridewells, productivity was the key. They had treadmills, for powering the machines that did the milling, and these were still in use at the end of the nineteenth century. Our most detailed records of this come in reports of visiting magistrates.

In the reports, manufacturers and businessmen from the locality are often involved, and a typical account of the prison labour is in this document, for example, in which plans are being made for inmates to be at work in woollen manufacture:

to employ two of the youngest and ablest constantly in combing wool who will be directed by two of his own ablest workmen ... the rest be in their number great or small will be employed in their separate rooms in preparing warps for shags, tummies, bindings, girth webs – or any other kind of worsted goods most profitable for the Governor to make ... The women will be taught to spin worsted if they cannot be made useful in some other parts of the manufactory.

In other words, the prisons were factories. Furthermore, the thought of working on the treadwheel for long hours proved, in the words of one report, to 'deter many from returning to prison'.

Nevertheless, there was education of some kind. Most local gaols provided a minimal amount of basic education. In most returns and inspections there is mention of elementary schooling. One chaplain reported to an enquiry:

The present schoolmaster and schoolmistress were previously officers of the prison, and were at my suggestion appointed to their present positions. Subsequent experience convinces me that I was right in recommending them to the magistrates.

The schoolmaster in one gaol, in 1853

> *is engaged to attend school 4 hours daily; he also attends the chaplain when on duty, and distributes books to the prisoners; the remainder of his time is at the disposal of the Governor for the general duties of the prison.*

We may see from this that teaching was hardly a priority in the regime.

Governors, magistrates and matrons

In the bridewells, the governor was a very powerful man. Back in the Georgian and Victorain times of course, the office was for men. He was often an ex-military man (see below at Northallerton) with knowledge of how to run a regiment. The reasons for this are obvious. A prison has to run efficiently and according to set rules. Even today, the words 'establishment' and regime' figure in the vocabulary of organisation and control which are essential to the success of the management of a prison.

The Georgian age was a time when sinecures were prolific and people were often appointed to responsible and powerful positions in society for large amounts of pay and with very little to do. The *Red Book* of 1820 listed 'pensions, sinecures, places, compensations and emoluments' in society, and this lists several categories of such positions, such as W. Adams, who was appointed General Commander of the Lottery Office at £200 a year (a six-figure sum now). Very few prison governors are found on those lists, and that must tell us something important about the office.

The governor was involved in all decisions. He could delegate of course, but in important matters, he figured prominently. Research into a prisoner ancestor who was in trouble for being 'refractory' as the Victorians put it, will show that the governor was involved where needed to impose punishment and make the important decisions.

The only people who could influence him were the visiting magistrates: this team were involved in all important inspections and reports, as well as in innovations and reform. They handled the finance and had most influence when change was asked for.

The governor at Lincoln Georgian prison, which is within the walls of Lincoln Castle, was John Merryweather from 1799 into the 1830s. His character may be understood from the fact that in around 1820 he was unpopular locally as he used prisoner labour when architect Robert Smirke's work was undertaken. This was in preference to employing local tradesmen. Merryweather had a salary of £300 a year – a very large sum then.

It is hard to generalise on governors across the land, but certainly, in reports of visitors, there is ample evidence that many could be humane and generous. Merryweather, for instance, earned this report from a Mr Neild, who wrote a series of prison reports which were printed in the *Gentleman's Magazine* over several issues in 1805–06:

> *I can form, by long practice, a tolerably good judgement of a gaoler from the countenance of his prisoners. Complacency and good order were visible in every part of this well-regulated gaol, a sure proof that the keeper is intelligent and humane.*

The matron was also very influential and had a great responsibility. In a system in which only very basic medical provision is possible, she is the focus of all care in the establishment. In the prison books and journals, discussed in Chapter 6, it may be seen that she had to cope with not only the everyday nutrition and care of her charges, but also with extreme situations such as handling condemned inmates, dealing with what we would now call 'special diets' and being sensitive to such ill-defined matters as mental illness and anxiety. She also handled drugs and medicines.

Case study: Northallerton – Bridewell to local gaol

We know a great deal about the gaol from its inception in the late eighteenth century through to its radical development between 1848 and 1852, as it had to cope with far too many prisoners to accommodate with safety. It can boast that it was the first custom-built gaol in England. That means that if we leave castle prisons out of the reckoning, the foundation for Northallerton gaol in 1783 is significant in the history of penal records.

As with all county local gaols, there were many facilities existing before that date in order that the justices had somewhere to send felons as well as debtors. The site for the prison was on waste ground to the east of Zetland Street, granted by the Bishop of Durham, John Egerton. The proviso was that his bishop's court should be held there as well as the local courts for summary offences and the magistrates' court to deal with felons. One of the town's first historians, Ingledew, explains that the land was low and swampy; it contained the town rubbish dump and a pinfold – the area where stray cattle were impounded from the common land. Dr Neild, writing in 1802, left us a description of the house of correction:

> *This prison for the North Riding is removed from Thirsk and has been built for about 20 years. The Sessions House under which are the jailers*

apartments adjoins. The whole is nearly enclosed by a boundary wall. The building has a double front and each has a spacious and airy court so that the sexes are completely separate ...

There was a vegetable garden and a wash house; then for prisoners there were twelve cells around four yards square and divided from each other by a passage two yards wide. It is notable that two of the cells were solitary: this means that the notion of what were officially called 'refractory cells' was there from an early date. Often called dark cells, these were tiny places which were one of the key elements in the later conception of prisons as places of a punitive regime, before the nationalisation of prisons in 1877. Men could be placed in these cells for days or even weeks in a space just 12 feet by five feet six inches by twelve feet high, or in the worst of all, which was only seven feet by five feet six and eleven feet high.

The place also had a large workroom (used as a chapel on Sundays) and another workroom of quite a large size. On the upper storey were the cells for women and the 'bell room' where the turnkey lived. There were five cells for women.

By 1800 it had been changed further: because there was a courthouse within, a large area was made outside and there were jury rooms and magistrates' rooms added. It was long overdue; in earlier years there had been sessions held at the Guild Hall (which became the town workhouse by 1800) and then at Vine House from 1720.

The new house of correction was not ready to receive its first prisoners until 1788. In 1771 the prison reformer, John Howard, had published his seminal work, *The State of the Prisons,* and although it happened slowly, there was pressure for reform at the local level. The first prisoners at the new venue were taken there from Thirsk; they were coming to a gaol that was to be a 'going concern' as well as a prison. It was to be controlled by a committee of visiting justices who would inspect and present their reports to the Quarter Sessions. From their minutes we can glean very interesting information, such as this entry from 1788:

Ordered that sacks be made of Harden [a fabric made from flax or hemp] *to be filled with straw for bedding to fit the bedsteads of the different cells according to the pattern already made by Thomas Winspear. That a blanket and rug be provided for each of the beds according to the pattern produced by John Marshall.*

In 1805, when most of the population were thinking of Napoleon or the price of bread, Neild came to Northallerton and wrote this summary, a very useful picture of the establishment seen through an objective viewpoint:

Thomas Shepherd, Keeper, salary £70, fees two shillings and for removal of transports one shilling per mile. Chaplain, Rev. Mr Wilkinson, salary £20, duty, prayers and sermons on Sundays. Surgeon, Mr Dighton, salary, none; makes a bill. Allowance seven pence a day. Number of prisoners Sept. 4 1802, sixteen ...

At one end of the prison is a small courtyard with a wash-house and bath, with a door for men and women alternately. On the ground floor there are twelve cells about four yards square, two of which are solitary, with a cylinder in each door; they are divided from each other by a small passage of two yards wide, which has a window at one end: at the other end is a large work-room, used on Sundays as a chapel, where the Rules and Orders for the government of the prison are conspicuously hung up. There is likewise another work-room eight yards square. A German stove in the lobby conveys warmth to this part of the prison. On the upper storey are two spacious rooms, one to work in, and the other, called the bell room for the turnkey; here the women have five sleeping cells and a work room, the same size as the men's, and divided by a passage two yards wide. The North Riding allows plank-bedheads, with straw in ticking, two blankets and a coverlit. The cells have arched roofs but are badly ventilated. I found the prison very clean.

If we look at other reports of gaols in Neild's survey, we find places with awful conditions; Northallerton comes out very well in the reports, though these were unofficial. The picture we have from this is of almost a family-size community, with plenty of space and good facilities. Neild's account suggests a workable, focused prison establishment with provisions for self-sufficiency and a watchful eye on gender relations. The costs also convey the strains on the budget – the costs of transporting convicts was very high, for instance, as the journey would have been to Hull or even sometimes to East Anglia. The professionals' income was comfortable indeed, though they took their responsibilities seriously, according to the later inspections.

Neild's survey was done as a commission from his editor, around thirty years after the celebrated survey by John Howard, so Neild had something to go on, and would have had few surprises. Yet we have to notice that there is only one criticism in his report.

The prisoners in this early period usually arrived in a state of dishevelment and often disease; they desperately needed new clothes, and from the very beginning a standard issue of garments was prepared: men were to wear a jacket, waistcoat, trousers and cap, the order specifying 'the right side to be made of blue kersey stuff and the left side of the same sort of material of a brown drab colour'. The women wore a jacket and petticoat, again mixing blue and drab. Comfort was not the main concern: kersey was a coarse cloth, usually ribbed; drab was simply undyed cloth, used so often that it became a 'colour' in its own right, used by all kinds of working people.

As to the plans for the prison itself, at this point a famous name enters the Northallerton story: John Carr designed the foundation and he gave himself most creativity and delight in conceiving of the governor's house and the sessions house. The cost of all the building work was £3411.3.11. The brickwork for all the walls, rooms and hospital establishment was £1372. Carr built Harewood House near Leeds and Fairfax House in York; the court house, session house and governor's house were completed by 1787 and George Parkin was appointed the first governor. Carr was twice the Lord Mayor of York, in 1770 and in 1785, and when he died in 1807 he was worth £150,000. He was not always wealthy: as a young man he had had to stay in bed at one time, unable to go out until his one pair of trousers was mended and fit for use.

Parkin was keen to see some of his charges employed in worsted manufacture; the women would be taught to spin worsted and two of the youngest and fittest of the men were put to work wool-combing. In addition to this were the occupations of picking oakum, chopping wood and making mats. Picking oakum was hardly a light occupation: it involved untwisting old rope in order to make a substance for caulking ships' seams (or other uses such as dressing wounds). In the woollen work there was a variety of tasks available: preparing warps for shags, tammies, bindings and girth webs. Tammies were rolls of fine worsted cloth with a glazed finish and a girth web was a strong, broad tape used by upholsterers. As time went on the dreaded treadmill made its appearance. In 1821 the first mill was installed. The idea behind this was that men would expend excess energy while at the same time doing useful and productive work. Obviously this was exhausting. Pictorial evidence of some treadmills shows that men were reading while waiting their turn on the lowest step of the mill. They were only allowed to read the Bible and improving works.

The Northallerton treadmill caused quite a sensation after a Bill of 1824 in which it was stated that 'no prisoner before Conviction shall, under any pretence, be employed on the Tread Wheel, either with or without his consent'. The magistrates in the North Riding disagreed with that. They

A drawing of a typical treadmill, used from Georgian times until the end of the nineteenth century. (Laura Carter)

carried on putting remand prisoners to the wheel, and Robert Chaloner, MP for York, wrote that he severely condemned the Northallerton regime and he said that the mill had been most illegally exercised at Northallerton. Following that, Martin Stapylton, a reform candidate and a JP, went to Northallerton to see for himself, and he reported:

> *On my arrival, I found several untried prisoners on the wheel, one of which had merely committed on a charge of bastardy to abide the order of the magistrates at the next sessions, and also two others who had completed the term of their sentence and were only detained till the sureties required for their future good behaviour could be procured.*

When Sir Robert Peel was preparing his new Gaol Acts in 1823 he wrote to all houses of correction and his letter to Northallerton was detailed, demanding to know their common practice.

All work was logged in a daily labour book, giving the amount of work done; these figures were later transferred to quarterly books, with the additional information of costs included. Underpinning all this was the deep-seated cultural and religious belief that *laborare est orare* – 'to work is to pray'. This was something deeply entrenched in the English mindset and always linked to religious observance and the good life of the honest man.

By the time of the 1837 report on Northallerton, there were four divisions of wheels: three were on the ground floor and one was above. In addition, there was a smaller wheel for use by the women; but the wheels were not considered to be 'hard labour' – as the prisoners' and keepers' linen was also washed in the shed areas, the mills were very unhealthy places. The author of the 1837 report notes that, 'The wheel sheds are close and ill-ventilated, and the effluvia from the tubs made use of by the prisoners while at work adds to the evil.' On hard labour work, there was pay: a quarter of their earnings went into their own pockets.

Around the turn of the eighteenth century, two views of prison had emerged: one was influenced by the Evangelical movement and this ideology saw the basic sinfulness of man in society as a pernicious evil to be combated by Christian work of redemption. Work was a part of that fight to save souls. This is why the prison chaplain was such an influential figure. The second view was that a criminal was a social entity gone wrong: he needed to be changed by systems of punishment and rewards. For many, the new regimes appeared to be brutalising: a prisoner worked long hours and then spent time totally alone; if he or she was insubordinate or violent, they would be placed in the refractory cell. Cultivation of the individual as a social being or as a spirit capable of redemption into society was seen as a too ambitious ideal. After all, gaols across the land like Northallerton were forced to put control at the top of the agenda. The priority was useful and exhausting work and the maintenance of silence. The idea of the 'silent system' emerging in the Georgian period was that if there was no talk within the regime, then not only would there be concentrated work, but also there would be minimal opportunity for dissent and for the corruption of young minds.

Chapter 4

PRISON RECORDS I

Quarter Sessions to Calendars of Prisoners

Before we look at the mainstream prisoner records, it is useful to summarise the legal system and the process of conviction.

The criminal's history began at the level of the local magistrates, as it still does. But for former centuries, the quarter sessions records provide us with the best first-stage records. Here we meet our criminal ancestors as they were dealt with by the 'Bench'. Local magistrates were always the cornerstone of our criminal legal process, and if an ancestor was standing before the magistrate (or 'beak') then he or she will be found and named there before the name occurs again in the first prison record *per se*, the calendar of prisoners.

Quarter sessions records are disparate, and the place to start is at your county record office, although they are all described on the National Archives Discovery catalogue. But some records are in print. For instance, the publications of the Yorkshire Archaeological Society, for the Victorian to mid-twentieth century years, have some such texts. For instance, in these records one first meets such offenders as:

John Child of Conisbrough, labourer, for stealing on 12 Jan., 1638, at Greasbrook, two yards of woollen cloth and a pair stockings, value 2s 6d the property of Ric. Williston. Confession (Puts himself guilty to 10d. No chattels, is whipped.

John's case stops there. But consider the case of Ellen Flaxton:

Ellen Flaxton, of Carr, spinster, for stealing on 4th December, 1637 at Carr, £4 in money, the property of Helen Reade. Witness, by examination and confessions. (Committed to York Castle)

Here the paper trail begins. After committal, a calendar would be issued of sentences given at assizes. A typical entry would be like this, taken from the Yorkshire Spring Assizes of 1862:

MARY GRASBY, committed 8th February, 1862 – endeavouring to conceal the Birth of her male child, at Bishop Burtan, in the East Riding, on the 27th January, 1862 12 calendar months imprisonment to hard labour.

Finally, the prison issued a calendar of prisoners, with entries such as this:

Jane Snowden, servant to Thomas Richardson of Bishop Wilton, farmer, committed 30th day of June 1801, charged upon the oath of the said Thomas Richardson, with having been guilty of divers misdemeanours in her said service and particularly with having absented herself from the service of her said master and failed to return ... Ordered to be imprisoned fourteen days.

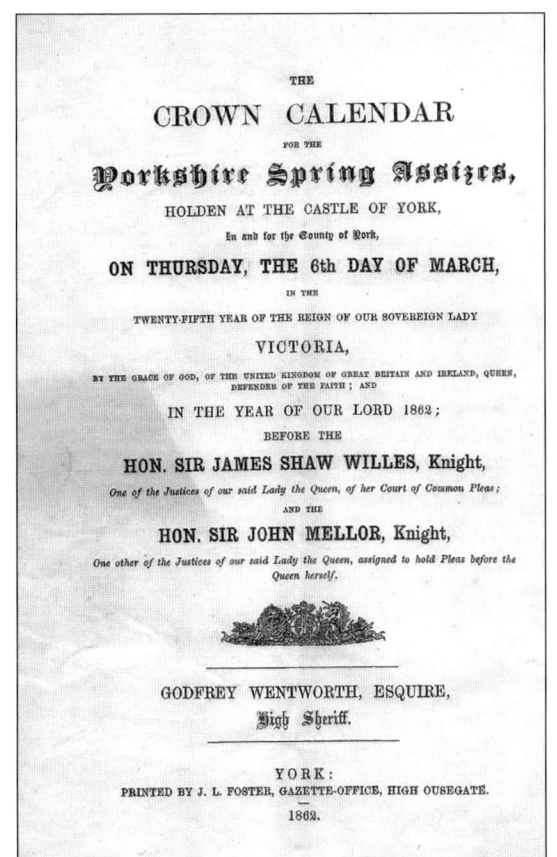

Crown Calendar document for spring assizes. (East Riding Archives)

However, in pre-nineteenth-century calendars, alongside basic details, fuller information often does appear, as in this entry from a calendar issued in Kent in 1640:

William Symonson He standeth indicted for deceipt in taking of 15s. Of James Gillen ... having no authority thereunto, which indictment he hath confessed and therefore is fined five pounds to be paid to the sheriff of Kent and is to repay the monies aforesaid to him taken ...

The entries may be quite long-winded and complex, but at least if an ancestor is recorded in this way, then a great deal about him or her opens up to scrutiny.

A similar entry from 1640 again gives a much more detailed than usual account of a trial outcome:

Richard Standen/John Salter These being found guilty of an enormous assault and threatening words to fire William Bowell's house, are to remain in gaol without bail for the space of one month and then to go to the house of correction and there to be maintained by their own labour for six months ... and afterwards to be returned to the gaol and there to remain without bsail until either of them payeth a fine of five pounds to the sheriff of the county which was imposed on them severally ...

The above examples illustrate the fundamental process: quarter sessions – assizes – calendar of prisoners. Every other record builds on this.

Calendars of prisoners usually give a clear and concise statement of what point in an individual's process of charge and destination is logged on the sheet. This is an example from an East Riding calendar:

A calendar of prisoners now confined in His Majesty's gaol, the House of Correction at Beverley ... for what, when and by whom committed, in order to take their trials at the general Quarter Sessions of the Peace, to be holden at Beverley in and for the said Riding on Tuesday the fourteenth day of July, 1801; likewise those persons who have been released out of the said gaol, since the last general Quarter Sessions of the Peace held at Beverley aforesaid, the fourteenth day of April, 1801.

It may be seen from this that the calendar is central to the legal process, and that there have to be post-trial calendars, found at local record offices; this document adds to the minimal details on the calendar, giving these facts about the prisoner: name, age, trade, degree of instruction, who committed by, date of warrant, when in custody, nature of the offence.

This would be a profile from long before the revision of the whole system in 1877. But in an important essay by Robert Shoemaker and Richard Ward (see Bibliography) it has been made clear that there was an acceleration of information-gathering in the early years of the nineteenth century, very much concerned with assembling abundant and detailed data on the working class, and in particular on state institutions. The reasons for this are many, but the directing power was for the state to know more about the growing industrial and urban populations. One factor in this is the arrival of the penitentiary. The first was Millbank, in 1816. The concept of the penitentiary, originating in the ideas of the Enlightenment with Jeremy Bentham and others, was that a prison should be designed in such a way that it would be possible for staff to supervise all inmates from a central tower, with wings radiating from the centre. It may be seen that these kinds of ideas indicated an attitude of total knowledge and supervision.

When Millbank was established, there was a chance to operate a testing ground for the theory of the penitentiary. There has already been a reference to the penitentiary of Onesiphorus Paul, a prison which had honeycomb cells; Paul's ideas were based on a system of regimentation and control.

Shoemaker and Ward's essay looks at developments in record-keeping: 'These developments in record-keeping and statistics were mostly the result of local initiatives ... revealing a grass-roots information-gathering culture'. Of course, this is massively important for family history research. The authors also point out that 'By 1860 vast amounts of personal information about criminals were collected,' and that a century before, there was little information collected, with most records limited to name and offence, with the sentence added.

We can see how the two factors match – the penitentiary and the new statistics – if we look at the thinking behind the new versions of prisons in the Regency years. Sean McConville has explained this very powerfully in his essay on 'The Victorian Prison':

> *For several decades prison administrators had experimented in managing penal discipline by means of 'progressive stages'. Breaking the prisoner's sentence into successively less restrictive and punitive parts was a feature of the regime at the pioneering penitentiary at Gloucester ... and this approach was adopted when central government set up its own penitentiary at Millbank.*

For the family historian, what this means is that more progressive and regulated sentence planning equals more paperwork, and so more prisoner records.

Consequently we have pre-trial and post-trial calendars. The pre-trial paper gives details of prisoners, and these are usually part of Order Books or Process Books as they are defined in archive listings. The pre-trial version is curtailed; for that mere logging of charge and committal what mattered was a document giving age, trade, level of education and the offence. A fully detailed calendar, from later in the century, usually has these headings: name, age, trade, instruction, committing magistrate, when received into custody, offence as charged, when tried, before whom tried, verdict of jury, previous convictions, sentences.

If we take an imaginary inmate, say Fred Jones, then the minimal information we need for the crime itself would break down to: name, crime as charged, by verdict, sentence. Thus:

Frederick Jones, larceny from the person, no violence, guilty of stealing, transported 7yrs.

Any other information opens up the context. Most commonly, for obvious reasons, we find 'Imp' in the column for educational status. This means 'imperfect' or semi-literate.

The period of the first penitentiaries came at a time when the local gaols were still operating, along with houses of correction, but signs of radical change are hinted at in the legislation of the mid- to late Regency period:

- 1823 Prisons Act : five different acts passed
- 1824 Prison Discipline Act: This, alongside the 1823 Prisons Act, brought about more regulated magistrates' inspections
- 1832: Abolition of the death penalty for more than a hundred crimes. These Acts had mostly originated in the so-called Bloody Code – a series of statutes that was mostly concerned with the defence of property, beginning early in the eighteenth century and extending up to the last decades of that era. Also in this year, the first prison for young offenders was created, on the Isle of Wight.

Sir Robert Peel was central to these reforms and new initiatives. He was Home Secretary in the 1820s.

Some of the wider elements in social history at that time also had a bearing on these changes. The Metropolitan Police Act of 1829 brought society its first fully professional force covering London. One specific Act which is significant in relation to the changing attitudes to crime and criminals is the 1820 Stealing in Shops Act, which increased the bottom-line sum of goods stolen, creating a capital sentence. This sum was raised to £15 from a mere five shillings.

An extract from a return by the magistrates at the Beverley House of Correction on the regime progress of some prisoners. (East Riding Archives)

Court and prison records

At this stage in the explanations of prison records, it is useful to note that they tend to be scattered. As well as being at The National Archives, registers of prisoners will be found in county record offices and some other locations, including the Prison Service. The information contained in these documents will not be uniform either: there will be variations in the quantity and quality of material found.

In any research into prisoners, there is always a feeling of detective work. This is because some records have disappeared, and also because prisoners were sometimes transferred across judicial systems, the most common reason being mental illness or a transferral for reasons of hard labour, or from prison to reformatory.

There is also an important point about the link between the location of the trial and the prison destination of the convicted ancestor. A classic example is the neighbouring prisons of Lincoln and Nottingham. For various reasons, a person tried at one place, in one particular county assize court, may be delivered to gaol at another place. This is why, at this point, a special explanation is needed about the initial search, usually on the internet, for a prisoner.

To illustrate this, imagine this sequence of 'detective work' about our fictional Frederick Jones:

1. A search begins at Lincoln assizes for an ancestor who committed a homicide.
2. The researcher decides on probable or known dates and does a 'sweep' with the search term 'Frederick Jones, Lincoln assizes'
3. Jones is found and the press report is found online at Times Digital Archive
4. The trial is reported and the verdict of guilty given. Jones is imprisoned.
5. This initiates a visit to Lincoln archives to consult prison registers.
6. Dead end.

The most likely problem here is that Jones went to Nottingham prison. Of course, the calendar will most likely note that Jones went to Nottingham after the assize.

Debtors' prisons

For close insights into the conditions and workings of debtor's prisons, it is rewarding to read Charles Dickens's accounts as he knew them well, largely due to the fact that his father, John, was a guest of Her Majesty in the Marshalsea.

A letter dated 28 December 1836, written by a certain Edward Fullbrook, a debtor, came to light in 2016, and in that text we have a narrative of a man not only in debt, but also in mental confusion and experiencing obsessive thoughts. Clearly, debt and mental stress go together. His letter includes drawings, and a plan of the prison yard where he was locked up at Oxford Castle prison. He also drew banners with words such as 'I love King's College Oxford'.

Mr Fullbrook is documented in the *London Gazette*, where insolvent debtors were listed. In October 1839, we find 'the matter of a petition filed on behalf of Edward Fullbrook, formerly of Summertown, St Giles … being a person of unsound mind, and a prisoner in the gaol of Oxford castle …' As he was mentally unbalanced, he could be released. This kind of document, which can be found by sheer serendipity in a search of criminal records, highlights the plight of imprisoned debtors. The poor man missed his favourite music and his times of prayer, and around him were 'inmates gaming and playing cards'.

For centuries, debtors mixed with convicted prisoners. Just like today, becoming deep in debt through credit was very common. Once again, the tireless reformer John Howard provides us with some facts, which are very enlightening in this context:

Debtors crowd the gaols (especially those in London) with their wives and children. There are often by these means, ten or twelve people in a middle-sized room; increasing the danger of infection and corrupting the morals of children.... Yet the little probability there is of an industrious woman being of much service to her family in a prison; the number of men in the same room; and of lewd women admitted under the name of wives; proves that this affair needs some regulation ...

Howard also points out that in 1776, in five London prisons these were the numbers in common categories:

Debtors	Felons etc.	Petty Offenders	Total
1274	228	194	1696

It is obvious that debtors behind bars were a problem.

Huge numbers of debtors filled the local gaols in the centuries before the nineteenth-century reforms; once inside the prison, the debtor would most likely find him or herself stuck in a limbo in which the production of goods with value would be the only way out, apart from hard cash.

The source of the debtor problem was the easy availability of credit for the middle and upper classes. Aristocrats and the new rich were expected to operate credit accounts with tradesmen and professional people. But working class families also often relied on credit to survive. One astonishing fact is given by Ruth Paley and Simon Fowler in their book, *Family Skeletons*: 'W.H. Whitelock, the registrar of Brimingham County Court, wrote in 1914 that there was "little doubt that 70 per cent to 80 per cent of working class families still supply their requirements on credit."'

Debtor ancestors in some gaols were carefully supervised and, indeed, protected. The key word here is 'contamination'. The managers of prisons were only too aware of the dangers of seasoned convicts being bad influences on new and innocent inmates. Rules for the care of debtors were spelled out in a number of statutes, including one of 1791. Some of the protective measures give us a meaningful insight into prison regimes at the time as in this example from Maidstone Gaol in 1820:

Debtors inclined to work may on application to the keeper be employed and will in such cases be entitled to half of their earnings and the risk and trouble of selling the goods shall rest with the county ...

Visitors to debtors shall be admitted to their visiting rooms from ten o'clock in the morning till four in the afternoon except on Sundays, Christmas Day and Good Friday ...

Debtors had a certain freedom of movement. Some could leave the gaol in daylight hours, carry on with work or meet with their families, and return, in the manner of a curfew, later in the day.

For tracing debtor ancestors, a useful general 'sweep' for any period of years you may have to start with, is often productive. Online, the key general listing is found in 'Insolvent Debtors' which were first published in the *London Gazette* and then reproduced in many local papers. This public record still exists, and as the website puts it, its beginnings were related to hearsay and scandal:

> *During the seventeenth century, potentially reckless publishing of articles – often just scurrilous rumours issued in pamphlet form – was thought to endanger national security, and this led to a climate in which the printing of any news not pertaining to the coverage of events abroad, natural disasters, official royal declarations and the most sensationalist of crime reporting, was largely prohibited.*

In that atmosphere, the news providers in print were in a mess, and after the censorship legislation was established in 1663, there were further problems. From the disorder and uncertainty of news generation came the official publication, the *London Gazette*. One of its many functions was to list bankrupts and insolvent debtors. The extent of the *Gazette's* material may be seen from one example. In 1769 a list of persons was published:

> *being prisoners for debt in the respective prisons [in this case, the South West] do hereby intend to take the benefit of an Act of Parliament passed in the ninth year of the reign of his present Majesty King George the Third, entitled, An Act for the Relief of Insolvent Debtors ... at the next general Quarter or General Sessions of the Peace ...*

The printed list covers, for the county of Devon, twenty-nine people, and from Exeter, three more debtors. It becomes clear that debt was always just around the corner, very close to the ordinary working lives of the masses.

The National Archives gives the reader a research guide for debtors. It also links to registers of creditors' petitions from after 1869, which have details of hearings in London and also records of the prisons dedicated solely to debtors, such as the Fleet.

There are also the prison registers for debtors to consider. As the London prisons of Fleet, Marshalsea and King's Bench were the main prisons for debtors, help is needed, and very helpfully Ancestry.co.uk has a page where a search for debtors in those London gaols may be undertaken.

In *The Bankrupt Directory*, which only covers the years 1820 to 1843 on Findmypast, we have over 30,000 records. These were taken from a publication by George Elwick. Ultimately, the *London Gazette* is the source of a large proportion of these documents.

Outside London, there are an increasing number of records coming online, and an outstanding example is the York Castle Prison Database. This covers over 5,000 prisoners between 1709 and 1813.

There is also the persistent problem of reading the records. The vocabulary of documents relating to debt is resistant to plain reading. Legal documents defining the situation of a debtor and his creditor also present difficulties. This extract is from a document which describes a young soldier in the Coldstream Guards, in the 1790s, and illustrates the problem. The prisoner is Charles Sheffield, an ensign. He is in debt to a Mr Spencer, and Charles's only real asset is his annuity, and of course his pay from the Guards:

> *and this deponent further saith that he this deponent shall and will at all times hereafter so long as the said William Spencer shall have any demand on this deposition, said pay in respect of the said annuity, have a sufficient part of their deponent's subsistence money in the hands of Messrs Mogrich and Porter ...*

Lincoln assizes. The debtors would have been in the prison, to the left, close to the assizes, centre (still used now). (Author's collection)

In other words, the ensign's earnings were assigned to a lawyer. The creditor wanted to be sure that he got his money back before the ensign could gamble or spend it all. The reader needs to know that the 'deponent' is the person swearing that the debt is owed. Wider knowledge is also needed, such as the nature of the annuity and how, at the time, it could be used to settle a debt.

Case study: Wesley Senior behind bars
Today, a walk around the interior of Lincoln Castle and its prison buildings gives little idea of what the Georgian prison would have looked like. But part of that prison remains, built by the great John Carr, who worked on the exterior. Inside, the place was designed by William Lumby, a Lincolnshire man. In that inner sanctum would have been the governor, his relatives, and the debtors of the county. In 1705, one of the inhabitants of that awful place was Samuel Wesley, father of the more famous John, then rector of Epworth North in the Isle of Ancholme.

This fact might come as a shock to some, as it is easy to imagine the country life of a local churchman as being peaceful and comfortable, as he would receive plenty of local help, and would have his own plot of land (his glebe) on which to keep pigs or hens, or even grow vegetables. Samuel did have some of these things, but the problem was that he made enemies in his own parish, and these were so fierce and intractable that they virtually ruined him.

Both Samuel and his wife Susannah had blood links with nobility, and Samuel's Dissenter roots had brought him a good education and useful contacts. He aspired to write and to travel, and was always full of plans and schemes on a grand scale; at one time he seriously put forward a career move that involved disseminating religious knowledge and faith in India. He was always looking out for a more comfortable income, as his family was large; but he had a knack of making enemies. In his first living, at Ormsby in South Lincolnshire, he had offended John Sheffield, Earl of Musgrave by throwing the peer's mistress out of the rectory when she was making a social call.

When the Wesleys moved to Epworth, Susannah had just had her sixth child; it was going to be hard to make ends meet, and Samuel took an extra living, bringing in the nearby village of Wroot. But Samuel's awkward, unyielding and argumentative nature even caused a split between man and wife: Susannah would not say 'amen' after a prayer to the king and he sulked, sleeping in another room. This was a man who was to find that not only his nature, but also sheer bad luck, were to strike at him, despite his efforts to make progress in the world. Susannah, known as 'Sukey', was the daughter of the great scholar Samuel Annesley of London: she knew her doctrine and her Bible, but she also stuck to her principles. It was a marriage of two strong temperaments.

One of Samuel's actions that was clearly intended to find favour in an age of patronage was a poem in praise of Master Godolphin, a folio pamphlet, and this was noticed by the powerful faction of the Duke of Marlborough, the champion of the battle of Blenheim. Not only was Samuel made a chaplain of a regiment for this, but he was also promised a prebend (a payment from the Cathedral ruling body making him a canon); but both of these were to be lost in the terrible acrimony and vengeance wreaked on him after a political mistake.

Samuel's ruin started when he changed allegiances at a local election, first promising to support the representatives of the Dissenters, but then changing to support the church party when he learned of the aggressive attitudes of the Dissenters towards the church. When the electioneering and news of the rector's perceived turncoat decisions reached the Isle of Axholme, Samuel Wesley was in for a very hard time. When Samuel was visiting Lincoln he first had a scent of trouble to come, as he talked to a friend in the Castle Yard and was told that his own parishioners were hunting for him, and that one had said they would 'squeeze his guts out' if they found him. After this, a campaign of terror was launched against Wesley and his growing family in Epworth. It started with a mob outside the rectory and pistols being fired; his children were frightened. He was then arrested for debt, initially for a sum of around £30; his flax at home was burned, the door of the rectory damaged, and his cows stabbed. He was locked up in Lincoln Castle, writing letters home, knowing that his family were being half-starved and terrorised. In a letter, he gives an account of the arrest:

> *On Friday last, when I had been christening a child at Epworth, I was arrested in my churchyard by one who had been my servant, and gathered my tithe last year, at the suit of one of Mr Whichcott's friends ... the sum was not £30; but it was as good as five hundred. Now, they knew the burning of my flax, my London journey, and their throwing me out of my regiment had both sunk my credit and exhausted my money.*

Yet even in the prison, Samuel kept busy and pressed on with good work. He writes about reading prayers twice a day and preaching on Sunday. He was sociable as ever, 'getting to know' his 'gaolbirds' as he said, and writing to the Society for Promoting Christian Knowledge for some books to give away. The working of the law was simple and inflexible: a debtor stayed in prison until the debt was paid. But most men in Samuel's situation would have no hope of clearing the debt; at least he had some powerful allies. Making himself busy helping the less fortunate was indeed a charitable thing to do, as many of the poorer debtors would be there for very long periods, and some would be in irons. Things had not changed much by 1776, when the prison reformer, John Howard, noted that 60 percent of prisoners in England's gaols were debtors.

The most horrendous experience of the whole sorry time must surely have been the desperately tragic events of Wednesday 30 May 1705, when a mob came to the rectory, firing guns and drumming, in the 'rough music' tradition of English culture, under the window where Susannah had given birth just a few weeks before. Samuel had taken the child to a neighbouring woman who acted as nurse. This nurse lay over the baby and suffocated it in her sleep. When she woke up and found the corpse, she panicked and ran, screaming with fear, to Wesley and gave the baby to his servants; who gave the dead child to its mother. As Samuel reported it, the child was given to her 'before she was well awake, thrown cold and dead' into her arms.

Samuel's debts totalled £300, a very large sum then. He wrote about his problems to Archbishop Sharpe of York, who helped him, both with money and with petitioning for help. Samuel was in prison for approximately six months, after a Mr Hoar paid him £95 and the archbishop added more. Back in Epworth he learned how his wife had survived; she had sent him her wedding ring while he was imprisoned, and he had sent it back, but somehow she fed the family and kept morale high enough to carry on. She had had no money at all, and the food was mostly the bread and milk yielded from her glebe. But the poor man with a sickly wife and eight children had pulled through.

A profound irony during this period is in the tale of one of Samuel's most nasty enemies suffering a terrible accident. This was Robert Darwin, who went to Bawtry fair and fell from his horse after he had drunk himself dizzy; his fall dislocated his neck and forced an eye from its socket. Susannah reported that Darwin 'lived till next day but never spoke more' and that this was an example of the 'severe justice of God'.

Samuel's life had always been hard and eventful; he was orphaned as a child, and at school in Newington Green he had been a schoolmate of Daniel Defoe. It was at Oxford that he entered the Church of England. His other life, that of writer and poet, is not much known, but as much of his work was burned in a fire at the rectory, it is difficult to assess his ability, and we can only say that a few of his hymns will live on in

The old prison within Lincoln Castle preceded the new prison on Greetwell Road. Samuel Wesley was held in the castle gaol. (Author)

Methodist worship. He died in 1735, at the age of seventy-two, wanting his son John to succeed him in Epworth. John, brother Charles and their friends travelled to Epworth to see Samuel before he died, as his time was near. Samuel's last words to his son Charles are memorable and typical of the man: 'Be steady. The Christian faith will surely revive in this kingdom. You shall see it, though I shall not.'

Chapter Five

PRISON RECORDS II

Criminal registers

It soon became apparent, when the prison reforms of the 1870s began to have an impact, that every institution had to have records concerning the people it held and cared for, even when that population might be an assembly of what many considered to be an 'underclass' best sent to oblivion. What emerged from this requirement, in mid-Victorian times, was the *register*. The word implies a simple list. In reality, it became far more than that. Even before the statistics-hungry last decades of the nineteenth century, prisons became, along with workhouses and reformatories, repositories of archives. Dealing with a human population means generating paper.

It is worth recalling that from the first decades of the nineteenth century, after the Poor Law reforms which began in the 1790s, what impelled social provision for the great tide of humanity washed up as the Industrial Revolution reached its zenith was an uneasy mix of philanthropy and utilitarian practicality. In other words, the population of the towns, swollen by immigrant groups and rural overspill after the relentless sequence of Enclosure Acts after 1801, created massive problems. This entailed everything from sewage and sanitation to health provision and employment, along with prison development.

Fortunately for the modern researcher, a fair amount of the paperwork generated may be in the form of a bundle. Often, at the court record stage rather than at the prison stage, something happening in an assize or at quarter sessions will generate documentation – at least, after the Georgian years in most cases. As the general interest in crime narratives accelerated (from around 1820 onwards), so did the realisation that sometimes criminal lives were of interest, and for a multitude of reasons.

The prison registers from 1770 to 1951 are formed by a massive collection of data, and these are from all kinds of prisons. The years covered comprise the changes in the prison establishment, first of all in the late Regency legislation, and then in the radical revisions of 1877.

There are also the Home Office Prison records covering these years, along with specific records for the principal London prisons following Millbank in 1816. Then there are the county prison registers from the main cities and towns; the information is often substantial, particularly after the legislation of the 1860s.

The information in these registers is mainly concerned with the data required in order to identify a man (more important of course before the arrival of 'mug-shot' pictures). Hence a lot of attention is given to physical characteristics.

There are a number of versions of the document. A *nominal register* may have these headings: gender, weight, name, age, degree of education, trade, date of commitment, name of magistrate, offence, place where offence committed, where tried, sentence, where born, place of abode, married/single, children, hard or not hard labour, number of times in custody, date of discharge, remarks.

The return of prisoners for 1878 in Lincoln has all this information and more. It also includes a list of punishments administered, and we know from this document that there were four punishments at that time:

- Whipping
- Irons/cuffs
- Solitary or dark cell
- Stoppage of diet

The *return of prisoners* material has these headings, as it is a basic statistical document on the overall regime: number of separate cells, certified cells, punishment cells, average number of prisoners at one time, daily average in half year, number sentenced to hard labour in one year, number sick, deaths by natural causes, total sickness cases for a year.

The remarks and comments provide specific insights into individual prisoners. These are typical comments:

> *varicose vein, right leg*
> Crooked nose. Lost 1st and 2nd fingers, right hand.
> Scars on back.

If we select one prisoner as an example, let us take Samuel Bishop, who was on the return of prisoners for May 1888 in Lincoln. He was convicted upon indictments for misdemeanour (false pretences) and was given three months of hard labour. Each indictment was to run consecutively.

These examples are taken from the years after the major reforms in records and management of the 1870s. As Shoemaker and Ward have argued (see previous chapter), this later period covered by the archival resources of prison registers was in a time when there was a wider development of an 'information state'. I will return to this subject in the next chapter when we look at the 'Digital Panopticon'.

The Habitual Offenders Act and records

The Habitual Offenders Act of 1869 made significant progress in the long-standing struggle by the forces of law and order against the high incidence of crime across the land. This was because the Act provided records of criminals, and gradually the offenders before the bench and before the judges had a 'back story': – a profile which had them logged and monitored. The 1860s brought, before this, the Offences Against the Person Act, which was a statute to reform and reorganise the capital crimes still running, and to rename and describe other offences.

The deep-seated problems of identifying criminals needed a radical rethink too. The 1869 Act did several things in this respect, but mainly it established a register of offenders, so that prisoners coming back into society had to visit their police stations and be registered. This was a time when there were none of the identifying instruments of forensic science available to the police. When the garrotting panic of the early 1860s put widespread fear of physical harm into the middle classes, the vulnerability of law-abiding citizens became most apparent. People began to see the importance of the police having records of known 'faces' in the criminal community.

Later, after the 1908 Prevention of Crime Act, a habitual criminal became a definable term. *Mozley's Law Dictionary* has this: 'a person who had, since the age of sixteen, been convicted at least three times of a crime, and was leading a dishonest life, could be convicted of being an habitual criminal.' By 1948 the term changed to 'persistent offender'.

What was happening, then, in the late 1860s, was that everyone involved in keeping the criminal justice system running smoothly saw the importance of logging and registering offenders, so that there was data ready to use which would help the investigation of crime, and also, perhaps more importantly, deter some offenders from pursuing their illicit trades.

Licences and parole

There had been another Act of Parliament, in 1853, which had had a profound impact on prison records: the Penal Servitude Act. This established the availability of a 'licence' for prisoners. We still have this today, and it allows prisoners to serve part of their time and then to be released under the terms of the licence. The value of this to researchers is significant. The licence in question tended to have other documentation attached to it in the records.

The licence was the outcome of a process we would now know as parole. Britain did not have a Parole Board until 1967, but in the United States it had existed in the nineteenth century. The notion of release on licence, regarding the British penal system, really related to the establishment of a *ticket of leave* which was given to transported convicts after a certain period of good behaviour in their sentence in the colonies.

The ticket of leave, which we will note again in the section on transportation in Chapter 7, was a document issued by the governor of the colony in question; it lasted for twelve months and gave the basic details of travel out to the colony and behaviour as a convict.

At the National Archives, at PCOM 3 or PCOM 4, the licence is usually stored with other documents. One such document there is the penal record, also known as a *caption*. From the caption we have all kinds of possible information about the inmate, ranging from punishments endured to medical history. Consequently some findings may be only a single form, while others could have a batch or bundle of paperwork.

Another factor is the tendency for licences to be broken, and hence the person in question is sent back inside the walls of the prison. The result? More documentation. But nevertheless, we have the actual licence itself, and this provides these headings: name, crime, details of trial, sentence, location on release, date of release.

If we look at the question of the bundle of related documents, then thanks to the organisations Ancestry and Find My Past, many of the related materials have been transcribed. A full picture of the ancestor may be assembled when these sources are put together:

- Census details of names mentioned in licence documents
- The licence material
- The court papers referred to
- Possibly the names found in the online Old Bailey Sessions Papers, which cover the years 1674–1913.

The full record of an offence has a long paper trail, and even in pre-trial materials, the names around a crime start to cluster. For instance, a subpoena, ordering a person to testify, will include names, as this extract from one in the eighteenth century shows:

> *Greeting we command you and every one of you that all other things set aside and ceasing every excuse you and every of you be and appear in your proper persons before our sheriff of Yorkshire at the castle of York … in a certain action now in our court before us at Westminster between Richard Clark plaintiff And Sir Thomas Slingsby baronet …*

There is also an archive of data regarding female convicts having licences of parole. This covers the years 1853–1871 and 1883–1887, and can be found at Ancestry.com. The Ancestry website summarises the case of Margaret Bannaghan, who in 1850 was convicted of robbery in Edinburgh and sentenced to transportation. She was paroled and then given a licence after four years. The important wording was that she was 'licensed to be at large in the United Kingdom'.

A profile, a shock and embezzlement

Prison records often lead to surprises about the nature of the life researched. Particularly before the habitual criminal records and the proliferation of a 'paper trail' pertaining to an offender, strange things could happen. One memorable instance of this is the feature on John Hurt, the actor, on the BBCs *Who do you Think You Are?* series.

John wanted to find out if his supposed Irish ancestry was true, and a string of disappointments followed as the family history work got underway. Everything led to a certain Walter Lord Browne who had opened a school in Grimsby. Then the truth was revealed, as the *Who Do You Think You Are?* website summarises:

> *Walter owned houses in Grimsby, to which he gave Irish names connected to the Marquis of Sligo. He also built his own school, which John visits, and finds Walter's picture in the prospectus, along with a claim that he had previously taught at the prestigious Cranbrook Grammar School in Kent.*

There was no evidence of that teaching, and what turned out to be the real story involved prison:

> *So off goes John to Customs House, to uncover a very different truth: the records show that William was a mere clerk, who ended up in a debtors' court and eventually a debtors' prison.*

The Browne story shows up something absolutely central to the nature of prison for debt at that time: it was possible to rise from the depths and get back into society. In the central debtors' prisons in London –

Marshalsea, Fleet and King's Bench – prisoners could spend time on a day-release system. We know a great deal about this from the novels of Charles Dickens.

At the turn of the eighteenth century artist and writer William Combe was imprisoned for debt and was able to go out to work, in daylight hours, to earn so that he could work towards becoming solvent again. Of course, John Hurt's ancestor was a different case, because he also committed fraud in the way he promoted himself and his business.

It is not only the celebrity stories that contain prison records that show the Victorian offender's ability to return to decent society after a stretch inside. The case of Henry Godden Garrett illustrates this. He was the second son of William Garrett, who was a lay preacher at Winchester Cathedral School. In the 1841 census, Henry and his brother William are listed as being with the family of Arthur Elzey, organist, who was working as a teacher, based in his own home. Henry later matriculated at Oxford in 1849.

Then, in the 1861 census, we find Henry in gaol at Derby for the misappropriation of church funds. Amazingly, he then appears ten years later as Master of Malton Grammar School in North Yorkshire!

The prison records for Henry Garrett include an *enumeration book.* This refers to 'the county prison' at Derby. Unlike other documents such as registers and calendars, this is concerned much more with location. The enumeration book has this information on the top sheet before prisoners are listed: parish, city or municipal borough, municipal ward, parliamentary borough, town, hamlet, ecclesiastical division.

As with John Hurt's Lord Browne, Garrett worked elsewhere, as an organist, after the teaching period. Thus he was mobile, acceptable and employable, in spite of his crime, which was embezzlement, and this raises an interesting point.

The researcher might ask, what was embezzlement, and was there something about that crime which made this social mobility and the return to respectable society possible? The answer is in the nature of embezzlement. Back in Tudor times, when varieties of larceny were being sorted out into definitions and descriptions, there was a problem with which offences could be defined as felonies. This was because tied to the notion of a felony was the phrase 'by force of arms'. The Latin phrase *vi et armis* (by force of arms) was applied to various types of larceny, but embezzlement, not involving such force, lingered on, as an awkward position for a court to deal with. In 1529 parliament tried to bring some clarity. J.H. Baker, in his magisterial *An Introduction to English Legal History* (see Bibliography) gives this explanation: 'The offence of

Convicted at the Assizes held on the 27th day of January 1883 for the *County of Lincoln* of the *Wilful Murder* of Mary Anderson his wife at East Ferry on the 6th December 1882 and sentenced on the 30th day of January 1883 to be hanged by the neck until he be dead, and that his body be buried within the precincts of the Prison in which he shall be confined previous to his *Execution*. *Executed* at 9 o'clock A.M on the 19th Feb. 188[3] *Coroner's Inquest* at 12 o'clock " " *Buried* at 5 o'clock P.M. " "

Present at the Execution

Henry Frederic V. Falkner. Under Sheriff
Edward Mackay. Governor H.M. Prison
H. Halford Adcock. Chaplain H.M. Prison
Edward Workman. Wesleyan Minister
George J. Mitchinson. Med: Officer H.M. Prison
Jas. H. Duncan. Clerk H.M. Prison
Henry Whitmore. Clerk H.M. Prison
John L. Rayner. Sheriff's Officer
J. Rider. Chief Warder H.M. Prison
Thos. Fox. Reporter Lincoln Gazette
George Kirk Reporter. Chronicle
William George Burcombe. Reporter Mercury
Charles Pickwell. Principal Warder H.M. Prison
Henry Boale. Reception Warder H.M. Prison
William Radwell. Assistant W. H.M. Prison

One gaol event we do have plenty of documentation on – an execution. (Author)

embezzlement as now understood, where a servant appropriated money or goods received from third parties for his master's use, was a more difficult case …' In 1799 embezzlement at last it became a felony.

The result of all this is that, even by Victorian times, embezzlement was a crime not only without force of arms, but also an offender could easily disguise malpractice as he was dealing with third parties in accounts and transactions within the business in which he or she worked. This applied to the Garrett case; in the Browne story, the offence would be fraud.

Case study: Police Court missionaries

In the course of his work helping criminals in London in the 1890s, Thomas Holmes had some frightening experiences. On one occasion he wrote that he had gone into homes in which wives were shivering with fear and the children ran into safe hiding places as violent men threatened assault. He wrote:

> *I have stood in front of these men and have been horribly afraid for my own safety, for with a poker or a hatchet in his hand, a man of this kind needs wary dealing. I know these men are mad but I know that no doctor will certify them as such …*

Holmes was one of the breed of unsung heroes who worked with the London underclass, trying to keep them from prison and a life of crime, years before there were professional probation officers, after the 1907 Act. He was born in Walsall in 1846, and he became an iron-moulder like his father; he worked in this trade until his early thirties, but he also spent time teaching the working classes, and after a serious accident, he was advised to apply to become a Police Court missionary, and in 1885 he was successful, being attached to Lambeth Police Court. Holmes later wrote two books on his experiences, and in one of these he explains that he actually had a moment of epiphany which led to his new life.

If your ancestor was one of the thousands of poor and deprived Londoners who found themselves on the wrong side of the law in late Victorian Britain, then the chances are that one of the missionaries worked with them and tried to help them.

As the nineteenth century wore on, the volume of petty crime increased so much that the old system of what were called summary courts were increasingly organised and administered by the police rather than by legal professionals of various kinds. A massive influence on this accelerating volume of crime was drunkenness, so it is no coincidence that the missionaries had their roots in the Temperance Movement. The

Inebriates Act of 1898 made it possible for the courts to send drunks to a reformatory, and there were a number of homes for inebriates. But back in 1876, when the Police Court missionaries idea was born, there was nothing to help women or juveniles on the streets, scraping a living selling anything from trinkets and matches to sex.

The human traffic passing through the police courts reflected the dismal failures of the affluent society of Victorian Britain, with its proud boast of wealth and progress, displayed in the Great Exhibition of 1851. Beneath the glamour and the expansion of Empire there was a growing class of people who found themselves before the bench for petty theft, hawking without a licence or prostitution. The police staff struggled to cope, and satires of the time, notably in *Punch,* revel in showing the swamping of the courts by the desperate and destitute. It is not difficult to imagine the chaos at the courts: a stream of people being brought in, and culprits in their dozens being loaded into the 'Black Marias' as they were shipped off to gaol; the missionaries squeezed in and worked when and where they could.

In 1876 a printer from Hertford called Frederic Rainer, who was working as a volunteer with the Church of England Temperance Society, saw this problem at the courts and decided to act. He gave five shillings to the philanthropists who were working in a small way to help offenders. The result was a tentative placement of two missionaries in Southwark by the CETS. From there, a quiet revolution happened.

After that, two former guardsmen, Batchelor and Nelson, became the first two Police Court missionaries. One snippet of oral history suggests that their friendship included one episode in which Batchelor saved Nelson's life. Nelson was in the Coldstream Guards in 1861, and was discharged with good conduct in 1871. In 1877 he listed his activities, and these included visits to 438 homes, 293 attendances at police courts and 149 temperance pledges taken. He made 117 visits to prisons and saw twenty women sent to homes.

By 1880 there were eight full-time missionaries in place and homes were opened. By 1896 there were six 'mission women' in the team, and in London, these staff would interview women charged at court. Some of these were sent to an inebriates' home at Gratton Road. The service of the missionaries was best summed up by Thomas Holmes, who said, 'Sir, I cannot carry Christ in parcels and distribute him. I can only do as I think He would have done … I give them myself.'

Holmes worked in the police courts until 1905, under the aegis of the Temperance Society. By sheer hands-on experience, he became a typical amateur criminologist of the times, working with the lowest and most desperate criminals on the London streets.

The missionaries went to extremes to help the fallen, the young ones destined to be on the police habitual criminals register. Thomas Holmes even offered his own house at times; he wrote that he dealt with alcoholics by giving them 'the shelter and protection' of his own home. Perhaps his most lengthy and heart-rending account of one of the offenders he worked with was that of Jane Cakebread. This poor woman, after a life of crime, died in Claybury Asylum and Holmes went to her funeral.

This does not imply softness and indulgence: on the contrary, the usual statement made about the aims of probation – to 'guide, admonish and befriend' – hints at the toughness required as well as the sacrifice of time, labour and personal comfort. What was very much a help and support to the missionaries, though, was the First Offenders Act of 1886. This made it easier to give the missionaries the task of supervising young offenders who had been bound over; voluntary supervision was undertaken for a designated period.

There was also a habitual drunkards register, and details of this may be found on the Digital Panopticon. Also, for specific years 1903–1908 these may be located at the Dorset History Centre, noted on The National Archives site at reference PS/PL/4/12. As with the habitual offenders material, this listed and described the kinds of people whom the missionaries helped.

All this needed cash, of course. A typical fund-raising effort was the concert given at Byculla Athenaeum, which raised a great deal of money. The missionaries themselves were not particularly well paid – around £50 a year was average. But progress was made, and some of the main achievements of the missions are very impressive, such as the boys' shelter at Bethnal Green in 1893, in which around twenty boys would stay and be supervised for several weeks. The achievements are best appreciated with a look at some figures: in the area of what is now Greater London, missionaries visited over 5,000 homes, wrote over 3,000 letters and took over 2,000 pledges.

There was someone else on the scene as well: William Wheatley. In 1887 Howard Vincent, a former Metropolitan police officer, saw through parliament his Probation of First Offenders Bill; this did not establish probation officers, but brought about police supervision with Home Office backing. The most significant result of this bill was established because there was a stipulation that the offender being helped had to have a fixed 'place of abode'. In order that this could be fulfilled, Wheatley set up the St Giles Christian Mission. This was before the Police Court missionaries could compete with this, and Wheatley began to collect and work with young men who had committed a first offence.

In 1890, a reporter from *The Daily Graphic* looked into Wheatley's work. His report included this information:

> *It was not always so obvious as it is now that there are more ways of reducing crime than by merely imprisoning criminals. A great deal is left top missions such as St Giles Mission to Discharged Prisoners, with which the names of Mr George Hatton and Mr William Wheatley have been so long associated .... The headquarters of the mission are in Little Wild Street, one of those narrow and not so sweet-smelling streets leading off Drury Lane ... But Mr Wheatley is usually found elsewhere, making his round of the prisons ...*

The missionaries existed in the provinces as well. In Cheshire, for example, a Police Court Mission Committee was set up in 1894, created by a clergyman, Revd Cogswell. Within a year, the missionaries based in Chester had been involved in 240 court cases. The first missionary employed was J.C. Porter, with a salary of £90 a year (much better than his London counterparts). The missions were then extended throughout the county, being established in Northwich, Altrincham and Stockport. The Chester Mission even extended its work as far as Wallasey and Broxton. Not all regions responded to opportunities to invest in this kind of probationary support: the understanding of the work done was slow to be disseminated, and of course, as it was always linked to church initiatives, there was perhaps a general feeling that things 'would just happen' left to the 'do-gooders'. In other words, there was not much in terms of organisational and corporate action to extend the work done in London in the early years. However, by 1900 there had been a definite change of gear in this respect and there were a hundred missionaries in the country by then.

In the last decades of Victorian Britain, the results of the Industrial Revolution and massive urban growth, together with immigration into London from Eastern Europe and Russia, meant that 'everyday' minor crime spread wider and went deeper: that is to say, as well as creating problems in the courts, this also added to penal issues such as the uncertainties about the prison system. In 1877 the prisons had been effectively nationalised and regimented, being run by military men. In terms of the efforts to provide help with rehabilitation, the emphasis was still on silence, reflection and hard work. Of course, until the end of the century, most local prisons had a full mix of age, gender, and population, nurturing what was called 'contamination' – first offenders being corrupted by old lags. Until the early Edwardian years, many gaols still had women offenders inside giving birth to children.

This wider view gives us an insight into how important the Police Court missionaries were. They reclaimed a large number of people who would otherwise have slipped into habitual crime, living in the sad and desperate underclass. Speaking in Parliament in May 1907, Mr Herbert Samuel moved a second reading of the Probation of Offenders Bill, and he made a clear statement of its purpose:

Its purpose was to enable Courts of Justice to appoint probation officers, and pay them salaries and fees, so that certain offenders whom the court did not think fit to imprison on account of their age, character or antecedents, might be placed on probation under the supervision of these officers ...

By the time of the Act, the London Diocesan Police Court Mission had clearly shown the way in this respect. The Annual Report for 1900 reflects on the nature of their work as well as their significant achievements. It lists the work done by thirteen missionaries: they had even paid rent and lodgings for 343 people, and the total number of visits made by all the staff – to home and court – was 8,319.

There were concerns expressed about the new breed of probation officers – which had never been raised against the 'amateurs'. Mr Stuart Worsley, Member for Sheffield Hallam, said in debate:

What deduction was to be made from the liberty of the person who was placed under the control of a probation officer? ...Would the probation officers have the right of entry into a person's house, and if not, why not? Was the officer to have the right of following a person about the country?

One might argue that this was a very English trait: to allow the good work to go on, with magnificent achievements, but then, when it was streamlined and 'official' and within a proper system, to start asking the important questions of both a legal and a moral nature.

By this time the missionaries were moving on. Thomas Holmes founded the Home Workers' Aid Association in 1904, and in 1905 became a secretary with the Howard Association. Even near the end of his life he was still helping others, and with a communal aim: in 1910 he created Singholm at Walton on the Naze, a holiday home for women in the open air. Holmes, Nelson, Batchelor and the others achieved amazing things in their work in the byways of London crime, and an understanding of their work gives depth and texture to any family story that involves offenders and their rehabilitation.

Basically, the missionaries played an important part in what we now know as probation services. When probation did come along in 1907,

Thomas Holmes, police court missionary and writer. (Author)

lessons had been learned. But for the genealogist, there is a bonus, in that the work done by the missionaries created records. In fact, some wrote their memoirs and gave the names of the offenders they worked with. In fact, the work they did attaches well to the new spirit of documentation described in my account of Du Cane and the new regime at the end of the 1870s. Their cases illustrate the aim of logging, assessing and then recording the offenders' lives and crimes, and then adding the conclusions to the general statistics and the police awareness of the trajectory of criminal lives.

Chapter Six

PRISON RECORDS III

Edmund Du Cane, as early as 1872, was worried about the quality of prison warders and other staff. He was a military man and had worked in the colonies. He knew that order and discipline were the markers of success, and the only way to run a community. He saw the need for prison visits and for closer supervision of the prison estate in all departments.

At the heart of his thinking was the creation of controlling commissioners, and also the formation of local Visiting Committees. What happened was that control and documentation came in, reaching to all areas of the Prison Service. In family history research, therefore, apart from the prison records themselves, there are the parliamentary papers, with their reports and enquiries, and there are also the local documents, describing conditions, just as were outlined in the earlier case study on Beverley House of Correction.

Du Cane was born in 1830 in Colchester; he attended the Royal Military Academy in Woolwich, and there his abilities in fortification stood out. By 1851 he was in the colonies, at a project in Western Australia, and soon he was working on land fort construction. When he was made chairman of convict prisons, he found his metier. As Bill Forsythe in the *Dictionary of National Biography* has noted:

> Du Cane was deeply sceptical about all projects for reforming adult criminals ... he emphasised that that the offender was a rational, cognitive actor, who must be made to know that the sure consequence of his or her actions would be the pains of severe imprisonment.

From a genealogical viewpoint, it was Du Cane who advanced notions of registers and documentation; he related this to the nature of detection. As Forsythe puts it, Du Cane:

> *defined every element of the regime in minute detail as to diet, labour, confinement in cells, rule of silence, worship, punishment ... release on parole, permitted reading material ... and so forth.*

In April 1878 the Prisons Act was established. As well as regulating the management of prisons, it established prison commissioners, and the streamlining necessarily meant the closure of a large number of local gaols. This is obviously important for researchers. Thirty-eight prisons closed, leaving seventy-five. What came in was the more organised and purposeful creation of convict prisons. When, in the popular imagination, a Victorian prison is envisaged, something like Dartmoor or Wormwood Scrubs comes to mind. These are convict prisons. More closures followed after further reports in 1880. By the end of the 1880s there were sixty local gaols left.

HMP Northallerton, previously mentioned, provides a useful typical example of the changes brought about in the 1870s across the whole prison estate under the influence of Du Cane. He took over as director of convict prisons in 1863 and acquired power over all prisons, including local ones. His thinking about the prison service was expressed in this way, when it came to matters of definition:

> *The distinction made by the use of the term 'imprisonment' to denote sentences of two years and under, and 'penal servitude' to denote sentences of five and upwards, no longer has any significance ... it is misleading, for both classes of prisoners are undergoing 'imprisonment' and are equally in a condition of 'penal servitude'. The only point to be kept in view is that the treatment should be adapted to the length of service.*

Regardless of definition, the basis of the system was still hard labour combined with a regime which would create deterrence. An 1863 Select Committee report found that penal servitude was 'not sufficiently dreaded'. Du Cane brought in a reinforcement of the separate system and the silent system: the 1865 Prisons Act dealt with the thought that many criminals were beyond reformation and rehabilitation. Something was needed which would make self-preoccupation a necessity, not merely something that was appealed to in sermons and improving religious tracts. Convicts were to be kept on their own for long periods each day; they were to wear masks so that they could not see other convicts. Du Cane told the Victorian people that convicts would get 'hard labour, hard fare and hard board'. It was going to be tough indeed, and there was no ban on the treadmill until 1902.

Between 1842 and the reforms of 1877, there were ninety new prisons built in England. As Northallerton was being enlarged, new prisons were built with a uniformity that would have pleased the Romans.

We can gauge the change that happened during the switch from local control to nationalisation by looking at the census returns for 1871 and 1881. In 1871 there were sixteen staff members living on the premises at Northallerton, from the governor, George Gardner, down to Annie Wilkinson, wardswoman. The concept of 'keep it in the family' was still dominant, as it had been in the early days. Mary Harker was listed as schoolmistress, but there was no teacher listed in 1881 after the 1877 Act, as the new teacher would have been resident outside the prison. The same applies to cooks and cleaners: in 1871 they were listed with the staff, but in 1881 the persons listed as staff were much fewer; those with an official occupation within the criminal justice system were included, and so were ancillary staff and the governor's family. So we have, for 1881:

George Gardner, 58	*Governor of HM Prison*
George Gardner, 20	*solicitor's clerk*
Lucy Norton, 57	*W Officer*
John Slingsby, 33	*Prison gate porter*
Alice Slingsby, 35	*officer's wife*
Mary Wright, 28	*officer*
Annie Moore, 34	*S Officer*
Eliza Topham, 20	*S Officer*

In 1771 the total resident staff numbered sixteen; in 1881 it was eleven, and one might think that in 1881 there was only one male officer in a prison with hundreds of inmates, of whom only eleven were female at the time of the census in April 1881. However, these listed people were only the resident staff: others living locally would have been at work there. Nevertheless, with safety and security in mind, Mary Wright and Annie Moore, one hopes, were trained in control and restraint. One can only surmise that the governor and his son, George, were very much 'presences' on the wings. There was no proper structure for prison officers at the time: it was still very much a family mentality, with the governor as the paternal figure, just as in the normal Victorian family.

The census returns also give us a profile of the demography of the prison. In 1851, just after the expansion and development of the site, we have young William Shepherd as the governor, taking over from his father, and his son had become qualified in law.

Gaol or House of Correction	William SHEPHERD 64 M Head	Governor of the Gaol	Northallerton
	Margaret SHEPHERD 61 M Wife		Northallerton
	Mary Ann SHEPHERD 39 S Dau.		Northallerton
	Samuel SHEPHERD 31 S Son	Barrister at Law	Northallerton
	James SHEPHERD 27 S Son	Surgeon	Northallerton
	Margaret Zillah SHEPHERD 22 S Dau.		Northallerton
	Elizabeth PEASE 25 S Servant	House Servant	Danby Wiske
	Jane COATES 19 S Servant	House Servant	Appleton Wiske
	Margaret SMILLEE 28 S	Matron	Caldercruix, Scotland
	Dorothy PALLISER 45 S	Wardswoman	Northallerton
	George HORNER 41 M	Lodge Keeper	Northallerton
	Jane HORNER 35 M	Lodge Keeper's Wife	Northallerton
	William HORNER 18 S Son	Apprentice Cabinet Maker	Northallerton
	Edward HORNER 11 Son	???	Northallerton
	William CHAPMAN 17 S Brother in Law	Apprentice Currier	Northallerton
	John PROUD 42 M	Night Watchman	Northallerton
	Elizabeth SMITH 11 S Servant	Miss Palliser's Servant	Yafforth
PRISONERS	William WARREN 30 S	Labourer	Blackburn, Lancs
	Mary Ann WILSON 24 M	Wife	Skiddaw, Cumbs.
	William JOHNSON 20 S	Labourer	Malton
	Thomas BAINES 51 W	Journeyman Weaver	Knaresborough
	James GETTING 40 W	Licensed Hawker	Sligo, Ireland
	Dotcher HUMPHREY 37 M	Labourer	Grimesthorpe, Yorks.
	James Jackson WARD 30 M	Gentleman's Servant	Carlow, Ireland
	John COLEMAN 21 S	Labourer	Annan, Scotland
	William McPHAIL 35 S	Journeyman Plasterer	Lochgilphead Scotland
	Partick GALLIGHAR 25 M	Licenced Hawker	Bradford
	George WRIGHT 19 S	Labourer	London
	Mary LEEMAN 36 S	Hawker	Armargh, Ireland
	Sarah HUNTON 50 S	Servant	Stockton on Tees
	John McADAMS 20 S	Gentleman's Servant	At Sea British Subject
	Thomas HORNER 43 M	Master Blacksmith	Thirn, Yorks.
	Thomas CRADDOCK 44 M	Labourer	Healey, Yorks.
	Chugrey TONGUE 18 S	Apprentice Blacksmith	Manchester
	Robert LAUGHLAN 18 S	Apprentice Baker	Dublin
	Thomas WATTS 30 S	Labourer	Matlock, Derbys.
	Francis SCOTT 25 S	Master Butcher	Rookwith, Yorks.
	Euan CLAYTON 43 S	Schoolmaster	Clun, Salop.
	Emmanuel FENWICK 25 S	Journeyman Blacksmith	Ravensworth
	William PILES/SMITH or TIPER 36 S	Labourer	Sedgefield
	Thomas MASON 25 S	Sailor	Hawthorpe, Lincs.
	Hugh BRADY 18 S	Labourer	Dublin
	William PICKERSGILL 24 S	Engine Tender	Osset
	William LYTH 20 S	Master Butcher	Scarborough
	Margaret GARRETT 57 M	Wife	Whitby
	James TAYLOR 19 S	Collier	Wigan
	Samuel BUCKLEY 17 S	Journeyman Cotton Weaver	Staleybridge
	Matthew WEBSTER 23 S	Labourer	Chester
	James BROWN 20 S	Collier	Wolverhampton
	John WILSON 28 S	Labourer	Dublin
	John SIMPSON 31 S	Labourer	West Indies, British Sub.

The census for 1851, showing Northallerton staff and some inmates. (Author)

The prison population at the time was 202, and the age range was from sixty-seven down to one year old (the child of a prisoner). The youngest actual prisoners were John Jamison, who was six, and John Appleton, who was eleven. There were also three teenage girls, all described as

A typical listing of basic details. (Author)

'factory girls'. Thirty-six prisoners were married and the most frequent description of occupation for prisoners was 'labourer', but there were grooms, tailors, hawkers, weavers, colliers and sailors within the walls. It is also a surprising fact that only fifty-one were born in Yorkshire. Seventy-one were Irish, and some from as far away as Somerset and Middlesex. There are many reasons for this, but one important element was the tendency for counterfeiting rings to be spread across the country, and there was a strong link between the East Riding and Birmingham in that respect.

Reorganisation and women's prisons

Early in the Victorian years, there had been no change from the previous Georgian practice of mixing men and women together in prisons. Notions of privacy did not come into penal thinking then; women prisoners were largely neglected and subject to all kinds of malpractice and exploitation. The turning point came with Elizabeth Fry, a Quaker, who in 1813 started to visit and work inside the infamous Newgate prison in London. She first established a committee of women, in 1817, and then worked hard to establish a group called the Association for the Improvement of Female Prisoners in Newgate.

With the arrival of the association, it became possible to develop educational and work-based sentence provision in the gaol. In fact, women and children together received some basic education. Fry's reforms began to grow and spread to other prisons; even the Peel-instigated legislation of the Regency included the fruits of her reforms, notably in the Gaols Act of 1823, which created women warders for the first time.

In the massive documentary work produced by Henry Mayhew and John Binny, we have a considerable amount of information on the lives of female convicts, notably at Holloway, the main female prison for the Victorian period. The authors give tabular details on the working day, breaking down the diet and the type of work done. Records from Holloway are held at the London Metropolitan Archives, with one set covering basic records and nominal registers for 1869–1984 (CLA/003) and some individual prisoner files for 1877–2012 (CLA/003). For the years 1889–2000 there are very useful governors' journals, committee records, prisoners' correspondence and Board of Visitors' records (B16/129).

The main regional archives have specific women's records too. For instance, at West Yorkshire Archives, Wakefield, there are online listings of all categories of documents, from calendars to nominal registers, for the years 1801–1914. For women prisoners held there from 1883–1896 there is a register and male and female prisoners are listed for the years 1801–1808. It is clear from the above that periods covered by prison records are piecemeal and patchy. The researcher has to expect limitations.

Only later, in the early twentieth century, did records of female prisoners begin to be separated, as women went to the new prisons especially built for them. This led to today's situation, in which there are a number of women's prisons across the country, with facilities dedicated to female needs and care.

Prison books and journals

Significantly for family history research, the 1823 Gaol Act not only established compulsory gaol inspections by local justices, but it also made quarterly reports and journals written by keepers, surgeons and chaplains compulsory. These items may not have always survived, but there are plenty available, and they are often very dramatic and informative. In matron's and surgeon's journals, for instance, we often find records of care and treatment given to the condemned, or to people awaiting transportation. These are the 'front line' professionals and they saw prison life at its most raw, brutal and remorselessly demanding.

The place to start, in order to understand the sheer spread and variety of record books kept by individual prisons, is with the most informative of the local archives' catalogues, and a look at what they have. I have been referring mostly to the Lincolnshire Archives and so I will use this again here.

The online listing is very helpful, in that it explains the description of the holdings, with notes on access conditions. The Lincolnshire Archives are like those in other areas in that often you will find, frustratingly, a note explaining Prison Service Order 1251: 'subject to longer closure periods. These include Governor's journals, Chaplain's journals and medical records all of which are subject to a 75-year closure period'.

Nevertheless, the same online listing describes what is there: nominal registers, index of prisoners, Governor's journals, Chief Officer's Daily Report Books, Registers of officers, all as the central penal records. Then, in addition, there are the records of charity organisations, a hospital prison and records of mental cases. All the listings have dates. Obviously, looking into Victorian and Edwardian material will present few problems, and the dates are always shown. It is the twentieth-century records that are difficult to access. Unfortunately, the journals of the Governor and surgeon are currently closed.

However, there are plenty of such records accessible in other areas. Medical documentation, for instance, is available in most places. Matrons and surgeons kept records, and in most cases, the prisoners referred to are ordinary people, typical of most individuals in the system. In the matron's journals for Lincoln in the 1850s, for instance, we have this:

1855 8 Nov.

1.30 Upon going into the cell of Mary Rebecca Douglas this morning I find that she is quite insane and to all appearance understands nothing. Reported to the Head Warder if it be requisite to send for the surgeon. Absent from chapel and the whole of the female prisoners. She is seen by visitor Mr D. She will not answer anything, she refuses food, the Matron has visited her four times during the night but she seemed quiet but moaning.

[later] She was very refractory. The whole of the female prison absent from chapel.

Surgeon's journals usually have ample material. Charles Gibson published his memoir of 'life among the convicts' in 1863. He writes of the people he met and treated, and among these was the notorious William Kirwan, convicted for the Ireland's Eye murder of 1853. The National Archives has correspondence and entry books relating to the convict establishment at Bermuda to which Kirwan was sent. In the records of the colonial office for the 1850s there are lists of relatives of the prisoners as well as some of prison staff. The entries, for the researcher, throw open a new angle on the convicts, as in this sample:

> *Patrick Dee: requests the mitigation of his son's sentence*
>
> *Catherine Foley: requests the remission of convict Charles Foley's sentence*
>
> *Mary Meagher: requests the mitigation of her son, convict Patrick's sentence*
>
> *William Watts: enquiry concerning the property of deceased convict William Hawkins.*

This shows very clearly that there is a whole range of related material about convict ancestors, all secondary to the actual prison records. The medical and governors' journals are the starting point for more enquiry. Sometimes the subject opened up is much more significant history, as in the case of the Fenian prisoners (including Eamon de Valera) who were kept at Lincoln, and the surgeon gives detailed reports on the treatment given to them.

The journal, as so often happens with daily logging and perfunctory tasks, opens up details on the lives of people who were important figures in history, such as this, on Michael Lennon: 'I ordered him to leave my room after he had made a disgusting and insulting remark regarding H.M. the King', and on another inmate, 'J. Milroy needed a dentist and a local man was recommended.'

The task faced by the historian is that of accumulating the material which composes the biography of the ancestor under scrutiny. All the secondary material puts flesh on the bones of the basic prison records, which give only an outline. What research really aims to enquire into is the crime in its social context, so that there is a grasp of the action of transgression and its many consequences, within the justice system of each period.

Scottish and Northern Irish records

The Scottish legal system differs from that of England, but when it comes to court and prison records, the formats are similar, and for the historian it is simply a case of noting the different terminology when it comes to looking for prisoners. For instance, there were burgh courts which dealt with minor offences, and, as a more general provision, there were franchise courts and these related to a franchise, owned by a powerful local landowner or similar.

The National Records of Scotland is the place to start, and the location of the central records of the Scottish Prison Service. The records also form part of the archives of the Prison Commission for Scotland and the Scottish Office Home and Health Department.

As in England, prison registers are the backbone of the records; a special feature of the Scottish material, however, is that some of the registers have photographs of the prisoners, and some have been digitised. A catalogue search soon locates the specific register for the area of your ancestor's trial and committal. The website lists all the prisons, from Aberdeen to Wigtown, and the materials are all at reference HH21; all the particular prisons are referenced at a number from the HH21 series.

There are some transportation records here too. The prison registers will provide the beginning of the trajectory, with the sentence length; then the record office has transportation registers for the years 1787–1870 on microfilm (RH4/160/1-7). The microfilm registers are presented chronologically by ship departure. The High Court records also have some transportation documents for the years 1653–1853.

To back this up, if Glasgow is in the historiography of the research, the website at www.glasgowfamilyhistory.org.uk has plenty of interest. Listed on the site are a limited number of particular records for a few dates, such as the police court records for 1813–14; the list of cases for the Glasgow Circuit of 1825, and criminal registers for Dumbartonshire in the Edwardian period. There is also a register of juvenile offenders who were whipped at the sheriff's court 1914–1944. For the years 1919–21 a register of prisoners also has photographs.

Overall the Glasgow City Archives has a helpful list of these, despite the narrow range of the material.

For a quick search of any name which might be in the records, www.scottishindexes.com>learningprison has a very efficient search option which covers crime and criminals, along with the wider context such as mental health records. This is all at the Scottish Criminal Database on the Scottish Indexes site.

For prison records in Northern Ireland, the family history search at GRONI (General Records Office for Northern Ireland) is a useful general start. This is a broad family history search, not a specifically criminal history search.

For obvious reasons, given the modern history of Ireland and the movements for independence, nationalism and radical initiatives, it is not surprising that the twentieth-century records have something special about them for researchers. In this case the example is the PRONI (Public Record Office of Northern Ireland) Prisons Memory Archive. As the website explains, this is 'a collection of 175 filmed recordings with individuals who had a connection with Armagh Gaol and the Maze and Long Kesh Prison during the conflict in and about Northern Ireland.'

For more distant past records, the Irish prison registers site on Findmypast is a central resource. Some information is needed first on the penal history of Ireland. As the Findmypast site informs us, 'In 1822 there were 178 prisons in Ireland. These records cover 3,127,598 prisoners who spent time there between 1790 and 1924'. We are discussing here a prison system which was working in the heart of a deep and ongoing conflict regarding Irish political issues, and about the fact that Ireland was existing as a part of the British Empire, in which Catholic people had no civil rights. Armed insurrection was a recurrent phenomenon. Prisons, in this context, were mostly local, roughly managed and had more of an attitude of repression than anything relating to the regimes in the prisons of the rest of the United Kingdom at this time.

The emergence of prison reform came later in Ireland than in England and Wales; not until John Howard made a brief report was anything noticed in that regime of abuse and mismanagement. In 1786 the Regulation of Prisons Bill was a first step in positive change, and in 1826 the Irish Prisons Act set up a Prisons Board and there was state control. The nineteenth-century Irish prisons were the panopticon model, the penitentiary idea again: perhaps the exemplary model of the new thinking was the Grangegorman women's prison, opened in 1836.

Findmypast has prison registers, as with Scotland, covering all the regional gaols, and the Dublin ones (Kilmainham and Mountjoy). It will be seen from this that the site and its resources cover the whole of Ireland, Northern Ireland and Eire.

Case study: Oscar Wilde

In Oscar Wilde we have not only a case study of a man within the new penal system following the work of Du Cane and others, but also a personal account of what life was like inside towards the end of the Victorian age. He wrote his classic long essay, *De Profundis*, about his prison life.

Oscar Wilde is arguably the most notorious English literary prisoner, closely followed by John Bunyan. In his writing he had a lot to say about the prison regime in Britain at the end of the nineteenth century, and in his *The Ballad of Reading Gaol* he produced a classic of prison poetry.

In his essay, *De Profundis*, he wrote:

While I was in Wandsworth prison I longed to die. It was my one desire. When after two months in the infirmary I was transferred here [to Reading] and found myself growing gradually better in physical health, I was filled with rage. I determined to commit suicide on the very day on which I left prison. After a time that evil mood passed away ...

We know now, thanks to the researches of Anthony Stokes, a senior prison officer at HMP Reading today, why conditions improved for Wilde in Reading. But he had had a terrible time.

Wilde's fall and disgrace are well known. His homosexual relationship with Lord Alfred Douglas, the son of the Marquis of Queensberry, led to a bitter confrontation with the Marquis, and eventually Wilde ended up in court, first after he took out proceedings against the Marquis for criminal libel (*libel* today) and second, after losing that action, when he was himself charged with sodomy. He was found guilty and sentenced to two years in prison on 25 May 1895. First he spent the weekend in Newgate, and was then taken by cab to Pentonville. So began his degradation. By the time he was moved to Reading Gaol he had experienced the worst of the prison system as it was at that time. Entry meant a strip search, followed by a medical examination and a bath; then he would have put on the prison clothes, with the black arrows, signifying that he was now no more than a chattel belonging to Her Majesty's government.

From the beginning, Wilde had problems with the food, and he was ill, suffering from diarrhoea. He could never really sleep properly; he was a large man and the bed was no more than a board with one blanket. It was difficult to be warm at any time. But he was, in some sense, a celebrity prisoner and he had friends who had power: one such was no less than R.B. Haldane, who was a prison commissioner. Haldane took an interest in Wilde's case from the start. In June 1895 he visited Wilde and promised that he should have books, pen and ink. Such a thing was forbidden, but as events were to prove, there were many aspects of Wilde's prison life that involved breaking the rules.

There was a furore on the part of the governor, but as is still the case today, there are exceptional circumstances in prison, and matters vary according to who the person is and what his condition may be: in Wilde's case, part of the reason for him having special treatment was that he was seriously ill. Deaths in prison are always embarrassing for the staff as well as for the Prison Service and the Home Secretary. With Haldane's help, Wilde got his books – fifteen altogether. Later he was to work in the prison library, and that was one of the most humane moves made on the part of the authorities.

Wilde was moved to Wandsworth in August 1895, and there his condition deteriorated even further. Concern was expressed for his mental health, and a doctor was sent to look at him, along with some specialists from Broadmoor. It was decided that he was not mentally ill, but the Wandsworth period did nothing but harm to the public image of the man whose plays had once entertained the glitterati of London. A chaplain wrote to the newspapers to report on the fact that, while having an interview with Wilde, he had smelled semen. In the late 1890s, when intellectuals were full of talk about the 'degeneration' of the human race, it was one of the worst things to happen to the man who was already, in the public opinion, the epitome of everything that was repulsive to the heterosexual, empire-building commuter class, with its dim view of high art and moral stricture.

When Wilde was transferred to Reading, as Anthony Stokes revealed in his book, *Pit of Shame*, his friends made his time inside much easier. At Reading there was an execution during Wilde's time: a soldier called Wooldridge, of the Royal Horse Guards, had murdered his wife. Wilde's experience of seeing the man, and in fact, of seeing the burial after the hanging, within the prison grounds, gave us the classic poem, *The Ballad of Reading Gaol*, in which we have the lines:

> *I walked with other souls in pain,*
> *Within another ring,*
> *And was wondering if the man had done*
> *A great or little thing,*
> *When a voice behind me whispered low,*
> *'That fellow's got to swing'.*

This reminds us that Wilde's spell in Reading was far from being paradise, but what he did have was a man on the panel of prison visitors who was instrumental in alleviating some of the pain of prison life for the great writer. We know from Stokes's research that George W. Palmer, of Huntley and Palmer the biscuit manufacturer, was one of the prison visitors. At that time they were known as the Board of Visitors, whereas today they are the Independent Monitoring Board, and their role is to tour their allotted prison and enquire on conditions by speaking to prisoners in the daily routine. The biscuit factory was next door to Reading Gaol.

Anthony Stokes's book on Reading Gaol and on Wilde's time there provides a fine example of what a prisoner's life was like in the prison system as it was reorganised after 1877. Wilde was subject to all the restrictions and treatments meted out to prisoners under the new convict system. Without the intervention of a commissioner who knew him, he may not even have had his books, and at Reading he was only allowed one book in his cell at a time, from a total of fourteen given to him by sympathisers.

Chapter 7

TRANSPORTATION

The historical background

A useful summing-up of the situation regarding the criminal justice system in the 'long eighteenth century' (as historians call it) covering the Georgian years, would be that it operated largely to protect property and prevent revolution. For all of that time, land and material wealth became central to the new commercial classes as well as in the ranks of the landed gentry. Their assets had to be protected. Short of establishing private armies, there was no alternative measure but instilling fear into potential offenders.

In Georgian Britain, when there was a steady expansion of country property and of businessmen who acquired great wealth, the rich controlled the law, and so statutes were passed to repress those who would aim at stealing any property from those who had it. Great wealth brings with it great fear. The man with a country house and hundreds of acres of deer park and woodland has to employ gamekeepers and other staff to protect what he has.

With this in mind, it is not difficult to understand the multiplicity of Game Laws which were passed in the eighteenth century to combat poachers; equally, these laws came hand-in-hand with an increase in capital crimes as the establishment sought to deal with rising crime. The haves lived in terror of the have-nots.

The plainest and most efficient way to reduce the number of criminals in the underclass and in the working class was to execute offenders. Many saw hanging as a terrible deterrent; the land was strewn with gibbets and gallows, as bishops and lords of manors had always had the facilities, as well as the power, to deal out a death sentence.

If we seek to understand the workings of the courts in Georgian Britain, this report from the Old Bailey in 1801 shows the inhumanity and callousness of the system when it came to dealing with felons, who were kept in overcrowded gaols, where they were likely to contract typhus and to live in oblivion:

> The sessions ended at the Old Bailey when 7 malefactors received sentence of death, Viz. Thomas Beck and Peter Robinson, for the highway; Dorothy Fossett for stealing two guineas from a person in drink; Richard Wentland for a street robbery; Anne Wentland his wife, for forcibly taking from Henry Parker 10l. [pounds] James Phillips and William Hurst for stealing goods out of a house at Hendon. Hurst was held up at the bar to receive sentence, and died on the back of one who was carrying him to the cells. The two women pleaded their bellies; Wentland only was found pregnant; 25 ordered for transportation, 3 burnt in the hand and 4 to be whipped.

Transportation presented a valuable opportunity for the criminal classes to be taken well away from Britain to work in the new colonies. An Act of 1717 stated:

> in many of His Majesty's colonies and plantations in America there is a great want of servants who by their labour and industry might be the means of improving and making the said colonies and plantations more useful to the nation.

There was also the settlement of colonies by workers and families. A work by Benjamin Martin printed in 1744 put the matter clearly:

> From a generous care and concern for mankind and a compassion for every distressed person ... the settlement of the colony of Georgia ... The design of the settlement was to provide a place of refuge ...

However, influential thinkers and writers saw the value of forced transportation. A reformer called John Oglethorpe saw and understood the desperate plight of a poor debtor called Castell, and he acted. He advocated transportation, influencing many others.

The option of transportation was always there, as a useful destination for lawyers to consider when it came to requests and pleading for pardon or for the saving of a condemned person's life. James Boswell, the biographer, was also a lawyer, and in one long campaign in 1774 in which he tried desperately to save the life of a client called John Reid, he wrote to the Earl of Pembroke to ask for help. In his letter he wrote:

John Reid was my first client in criminal business when he was tried in 1766. I have therefore a particular concern in his fate and wish much that he should not be hanged ... It would therefore be happy if a transportation pardon could be obtained for him at once ...

The plea didn't work and Boswell lost his client. The man was hanged at the Edinburgh Grassmarket.

Later, after the loss of the American colonies in the American War of Independence, Britain lost the lands previously used as destinations for convict labour, and so, after 1776, the system switched to Australia. In 1788 Botany Bay, near Sydney, was the new first destination, with other places being established later. The resulting developments were very important in the overall development of the British penal system. Estimated figures for transportation were given by the 1837 *Report of the Select Committee on Transportation*. That document stated that between 1787 and 1837, 75,200 convicts were transported to New South Wales. Soon after, between 1817 and 1837, 27,729 were sent to Van Dieman's Land, now Tasmania.

Plenty of women and children were transported. In 1947, S.G. Partridge gave a useful account of a typical sample of such prisoners, including this extract, to show the nature of the system. He quoted from the records of the convict ship *Elphinstone*, which sailed from Chatham in 1836:

Name	Age	Offence	Convicted at	Sentence	Trade
J. Patterson	14	Stealing articles	Liverpool	14 years	Shoemaker
I. Owen	13	Stealing tongs and 6 spoons	Liverpool	14 years	Labourer
W. Bell	15	Stealing various articles	Liverpool	14 years	Labourer
W. Blackmore	16	Housebreaking	Bridgwater	Life	Labourer
P. Nugent	16	Housebreaking	Bridgwater	Life	Tailor

When the emphasis shifted south from Sydney to Hobart, Tasmania, a site was needed for the more recalcitrant convicts, and so Port Arthur, on the isthmus at Eagle's Neck, was seen as the ideal place for a penitentiary and a cluster of associated workshops, chapel and other ancillary buildings. One handbook to Port Arthur, written recently by Alex Graeme-Evans, notes that:

Concerns as to the ease of escape to the hinterlands of New South Wales from Sydney Town, combined with a clear understanding that there were emerging two types of convicts (those that were amenable to reform and those that were not) seeded the idea in the minds of the colonial establishment in Australia that the setting up of a secondary type of penal settlement was now timely.

Today, there is a mass of information to help with family history research into this convict system. Not only has there been a marked expansion of listings online, but also regional and specialist organisations have printed material which is easily available. At the heritage sites in Australia, the publishing industry has generated all kinds of material relating to transported convicts. A typical publication is *Pack of Thieves?* by Hamish Maxwell-Stewart and Susan Hood (see Bibliography) in which fifty-two convict lives are told. Other publications even provide projected drawings of the faces of convicts, taken from the printed records.

Understanding the system and the trajectory of the convicts' lives is helpful at this point. Essentially, it was a probationary implementation; it started with advance notice of a ship's arrival.

When the potential masters of businesses had the listings, they applied for convict servants. Otherwise, the convicts were sent to a penitentiary, the most infamous being at Port Arthur. There were also other colonies, such as at Norfolk Island, off the Australian shore. S.G. Partridge provides a neat summary of the situation:

Labourers ... were assigned at once to agricultural settlers or other suitable masters, and in proportion as they were labourers and well behaved, it was not to the interests of their masters to facilitate their obtaining a ticket of leave ... When at length, their sentence completed, they did obtain ticket of leave, in order to subsist at all they might have to continue their labour in exile with no hope of return ...

What happened was that the probationary system, in many locations, worked by sending out parties of convicts to rural areas to do building work, where they would be lodged in smaller local gaols. In Tasmania, for instance, at Richmond (where the gaol is still preserved), convicts would be sent out to work building bridges and other public works, in work-gangs, with guards and overseers keeping a close watch on them. Today, close to the Pacific coast of Tasmania, convict-built bridges and roads may still be seen by travellers. The work was solid and made to last.

Three images showing a cell, a wing gate and a panoramic view of the Tasmanian penal settlement. (Author)

A county in focus

At county record offices and archives in the United Kingdom much effort has been made to make records more user-friendly. Using Lincolnshire again as an example, the county records of transported convicts demonstrate both the material available and the approaches to use.

First, for the family historian, there is the information on the website. The database is described, and all researchers owe a debt to

C.L. Anderson of the Open University, who produced a book about Lincolnshire convicts to Australia in 2000 (see Bibliography).

The guidance is a great help. Lists of possible problems are given and explained, for instance, referring back to the convict's court records:

> *A convict's place of origin may not refer to the place where he or she was born, or even where they lived, as the courts sometimes merely describe the prisoner as being 'of' the place of the crime.*

Also, helpfully, the website explains that the assize court records relating to specific prisoners may not be at Lincoln, but elsewhere, probably in The National Archives. Even more usefully, Anderson's lists were reprinted in a booklet by Lincolnshire County Council, and this has been retained in print. The following are typical entries:

Name	Age	Date	Place	Sentence	Origin	Year	Place	Ship
Burrell Francis	20	27/7/1816	Ass.	Life	Coningsby	1818	NSW	*Almora*
Baker John	-	17/1/1817	LQS	7yrs	Coningsby	1818	NSW	*Neptune*
Brady Eliza	33	8/3/1817	LQS	7yrs	St Child, Boston	1818	NSW	*Friendship*

Note: Ass – Assizes; LQS – Lincs Quarter Sessions; NSW – New South Wales

This is an actual example of a most typical offence, trial and destination in those harsh times. Similar cases are not hard to find if one searches in the Times Digital Archives and investigates the cases at Lincoln Assizes. For obvious reasons, offences such as poaching, arson and other rural transgressions led to a transportation sentence.

In Sian Rees's book, *The Floating Brothel*, she recounts the story of one of Lincoln's most celebrated convicts of the eighteenth century: Mary Rose, whose age at trial we do not really know. She could have been anything from sixteen to twenty. But whatever her age, the case fanned the flames of emotion and indignation around the city in 1788. The famous naturalist, Sir Joseph Banks, followed the case avidly, and a poem published in a local newspaper at the time has the lines:

> *Twas then my wandering thoughts did bend*
> *To Lincoln prison dreary cell*
> *Where weeks and months without a friend,*
> *A ROSE, distressed, is forced to dwell.*

What was Rose's crime? It began with a romantic elopement from Lincoln one night – the culmination of an affair with a young officer. Mary was a farmer's daughter, so there were several reasons why a marriage would not have been on the cards.

Everything was pointing to the fact that young Mary was to be a 'fallen woman' if she could not be retrieved very quickly indeed. The search was on: Mary had a reasonable income so she could have survived for some years even if her officer was penniless, but it was the shame and family dishonour. For reasons which are not entirely clear, the officer left Mary in her Lincoln lodging house. This is where the ease with which a respectable person could slide into criminality becomes clear. The landlady, a Mrs Kestleby, saw that there was money to be had from this situation.

She shopped Mary for a supposed theft. Off went poor Mary from the magistrate to the prison to wait for the next circuit judge. At the trial there was a good turn-out, as there were two murderers due to appear, and, of course, an attractive young woman. Mary could offer nothing in defence and the course of events was frighteningly speedy. Mary, along with some local housebreakers and thieves, was sentenced to be taken to 'parts beyond the seas' for her 'crime.'

Now we have to ask what her family did to try to help, and what Banks might have done. Mary was in gaol in Lincoln for eighteen months before any wagon arrived to take her to a ship. During that time her family brought her food and clothes, but time went on and she was more and more abandoned to an unknown fate. Until, that is, Joseph Banks stepped in.

Banks was involved in the colonisation of New South Wales, and a garrison had been founded and developed at Sydney Cove by the time this affair with Mary was in process. Banks did everything he could to have Mary taken to join this settlement, even paying out pocket money for her. Mary, for her part, did want to go there. Basically, the colony needed more women. It was that simple. Mary was an ideal candidate and so it happened.

Her story reads like a Hollywood drama at times, with her being such a dupe of a villain; it could also be a piece of fiction from Daniel Defoe. But the fact is that Mary Rose was a Lincolnshire girl who had an incredible adventure. Looking back at the story now, one wonders why nothing was achieved at the trial, with Kestleby so clearly superior as a voice to be heard. On the other hand, William Morris, a young man from Fleet 'was charged with feloniously stealing a horse ... and a pony' and was transported for life. Here was another man with no powerful friends. Mary, with some income and a farming family, could still not overcome the challenges and obstacles involved in the legal system of her time.

The Digital Panopticon (www.digitalpanopticon.org/Records)
For help and guidance with the search for a transported convict ancestor, this facility is unequalled. With a grant from the Arts and Humanities Research Council, a resource with a digital transformation theme was established, and now a valuable group of datasets are available online, generated by the Digital Humanities Institute at the University of Sheffield. These listings are on the site:

- Dead Prisoners Index 1800–1869
- Registers of Prison Licences for London Convicts
- Western Australia Convict Records
- Middlesex House of Detention Calendars 1826–1889
- Metropolitan Police Register of Habitual Criminals 1881–1925
- UK Licences of Pardon of Convicts 1833–1925

Court and trial records go along with these, including Newgate calendars. Regarding transportation, these records are included in the Panopticon:

- Middlesex Convicts Delivered for Transportation 1785–1792
- British Transportation Registers 1787–1867
- Convict Indents (Ship and arrival registers) 1788–1868
- Surgeons' Notes from Transport Vessels 1817–1857.
- Obviously, there is information needed for events and developments across the oceans in the colonies themselves, so the Panopticon has:
- New South Wales Convict Indexes 1788–1873
- New South Wales Convict Savings Bank Books 1824–1868
- Van Dieman's Land Founders and Survivors Convicts 1802–1853
- Van Dieman's Land Founders and Survivors Convict Biographies 1812–1853
- Van Dieman's Land Convict Labour Contracts 1848–1857
- Western Australia Character Books and General Registers 1850–1868
- Western Australia Convict Probation Records 1850–1868

The database does have Old Bailey records too, but here it is worth including something on the Old Bailey Sessions papers online. This covers the years 1674–1913. The material derives from publications which aimed to give fairly detailed accounts of trials at the Old Bailey (the Central Criminal Court). Today these sessions papers are online, and the sources and texts are linked to the Digital Panopticon, and there are more records on the State Library of Queensland database of convicts. Transportation to Australia ended in 1868 when the last transport ships set sail.

All the records provide information, but perhaps petitions for pardon tell us more than most. The Digital Panopticon offers a series of case studies to fill out the facts, and a typical one is that of Mary Ann Hall. She was born in Hull, but her criminal career flourished in London, and from a group of records, the Digital Panopticon assembled plenty of information about her, right through to her death, back in Hull in 1888. The records used were: Old Bailey Proceedings Online; UK Licences of Parole for Female Convicts 1853–1887; England census 1851.

The hulks

From 1776, the bright idea struck the prison establishment that damaged and useless former warships would make ideal floating prisons. In between trying to rest and sleep on the ships, which were rife with disease, the convicts worked on the dockyards, on construction and

A typical prison hulk craft at Deptford. (Author)

An eighteenth-century account of convict lives, in the era before Australia was opened up for use. (J.S. Turberville English Men and Manners in the Eighteenth Century*)*

> A SELECT and IMPARTIAL
>
> # ACCOUNT
>
> OF THE
>
> LIVES, BEHAVIOUR, and DYING WORDS, of the moſt remarkable
>
> # CONVICTS,
>
> From the Year 1725, down to the preſent Time.
>
> CONTAINING
>
> Amongſt many Others, the following, *viz*.
>
> *Catherine Hayes*, for the barbarous Murder of her Husband.
>
> *Edward Burworth*, *Wm. Blewit*, and five more, for the Murder of Mr. *Ball*, in St. *George's-Fields*.
>
> *James Cluff*, for the Murder of his Fellow Servant, *Mary Green*.
>
> *John Gow*, alias *Smith*, Captain of the Pyrates, for Pyracy and Murder.
>
> Mr. *Maynee*, one of the Clerks of the Bank of England, for cheating the Bank of 4420 l.
>
> Mr. *Woodmarſh*, for the Murder of Mr. *Robert Ormes*.
>
> *John Sheppard*, who made his Eſcape out of the Condemn'd-Hole, and likewiſe out of the Stone-Room in *Newgate*.
>
> *Robert Hallam*, for the barbarous Murder of his Wife, by throwing her out of Window.
>
> Mr. *Shelton*, the Apothecary, a Highwayman.
>
> *Sarah Malcomb*, for the barbarous Murder of *Ann Price*, *Eliz. Harriſon*, and *Lydia Duncomb*, in the *Temple*.
>
> *John Field*, *Joſeph Roſe*, *Wm. Buſh*, and *Humphry Walker*, for entering the Houſe of Mr. *Lawrence*, and Mr. *Francis*.
>
> *Fœlix quem faciunt aliena Pericula cautum*.
>
> VOL. II.
>
> *LONDON:*
> Printed by J. APPLEBEE, for J. HODGES, at the *Looking-Glaſs*, on *London-Bridge*; and ſold alſo by C. CORBETT, at *Addiſon's-Head*, oppoſite St. *Dunſtan's-*Church, in *Fleet-ſtreet*. M,DCC,LX.

repair projects; the Woolwich Royal Arsenal was always in need of labour, as were other fortifications.

The regime on the hulks was extremely tough, with a restricted diet being administered and long hours of work imposed. Henry Mayhew, quoted earlier regarding London prisons, made this note about one particular hulk moored on the Thames: 'The state of morality under such circumstances may be easily conceived, crimes impossible to mention being commonly perpetrated.' It was not until 1856, after a House of Commons Committee had reported on these ships and recommended their abolition as prison substitutes, that anything was done.

Lord Brougham, reformer and humanitarian, wrote of the hulks:

the utterly execrable, the altogether abominable hulk, lies moored in the face of the day it darkens, within sight of the land it insults, riding on the waters which it stains with every unnatural excess of infernal pollution, triumphant over all morals.

One hulk, the *Justicia*, attracted plenty of negative media attention, and as well as reports in print on abuses and terrible conditions there, the great artist George Cruickshank drew a picture entitled 'Death on Board the Hulk *Justicia*' showing three men lying in their beds, with one of them clearly just expired. A warder closes his eyes, as a despairing surgeon looks on, and two prison warders stand by to keep the scene out of general view, as if they are hiding the result of their application of abuse and cruel treatment.

One line from a metropolitan prison list conveys the horrendous cruelty of the system of retributive justice which prevailed in the late Georgian times:

No	Name	Age	Charge	Sentence
73	Thomas Evans	15	Felony	Death. One year's H.L, two month's solitary confinement, and then transported for life.

On statistical returns, there are hulk populations. In 1841 there were 3,625, and 1,451 of these were first offenders. That fact alone highlights the sheer thoughtless utilitarian function of the hulk and transportation system. Felons were lumped together, after sentence, then carried to hulks until their ship sailed for Australia. Some of the hulks were permanent, however; clearly, these would house the beast labourers for the dockyards and forts.

We know something of the death-rates on the hulks. In 1841, for instance, it was 7.8 percent per annum. The daily routine came out when there was a prison committee formed. In 1832 such a committee reported that a convict with the initials A.B. had this regime:

> *Rose at 5.30*
> *Breakfast at 6*
> *Left for shore 7 or 7.30*
> *Back for dinner noon.*
> *Labour from 13.00 to 17.00*
> *Lock-down at 19.00*

The fullest records are the hulks registers and the search term on the Digital Panopticon is: Hulks_Registers_1801-1879

Journeys and returns

Many convicts served their term and then, with a ticket of leave, returned to Britain. Such a man was Charles Moore, convicted in London in 1832 for stealing from a person. He was sentenced to transportation for seven years. In Van Dieman's Land he was not sent to Port Arthur but to Launceston on the northern coast, where he was a bound servant to a Mr George Hamilton. He was caught stealing and the punishment was to work on a hulk chain-gang.

He worked on the roads for two years, but then tried to make a break from his probationary time by climbing aboard ship bound for South America. He was found and taken back into custody, this time at Port Arthur. Although he was constantly in trouble for small thefts, he eventually, in 1844, was awarded his ticket of leave, and in 1852 he was on board the *Halcyon*, going to Melbourne. Moore's ticket of leave would have covered twelve months from the stated date. He must have managed to behave himself for a few years in order to have a ticket issued. A ticket would have looked like this:

Date: Registered in the Office of the Principal Superintendent of Convicts
It is His Excellency's, the Governor's, Pleasure to dispense with the attendance at Government work of .... who was tried at ....
Convict for .... arrived per Ship ....
.... Master, in the year .... and to permit
To employ .... self for .... own advantage during good behaviour
Or until His Excellency's further Pleasure shall be made known.

Case study: a Yorkshire family

Sometimes, it is the work of the social historian or antiquarian that opens up a criminal life. This is the case with an east Yorkshire family called Dunhill. In 1874, Sabine Baring-Gould published *Yorkshire Oddities, Incidents and Strange Events*, and in that volume he included a chapter on 'Snowden Dunhill, the Convict.' That author's source was no less than Dunhill's own autobiography, published in 1833.

Baring-Gould recounts, quoting Dunhill's own words most of the time, that after a life of petty rural crime, Dunhill was arrested and tried for theft, then sentenced to a long stretch in gaol. Dunhill has this in his autobiography: 'I was immediately conveyed back to my cell, and a few days afterwards I was forwarded to the hulks. In this miserable banishment I spent six years'. His wife, Sarah, was also imprisoned, at York Castle. Now, in Snowden's case, he actually wanted to be transported, as he wrote:

> *I had heard much of the easy lives led by convicts in New South Wales; and, moreover, some members of my family were already there, and I felt impelled to make an endeavour to join them ... I was soon traced to the commission of paltry crime and convicted; ... My trial took place at a district quarter sessions in the north of Lincolnshire [at Brigg, in 1823] ... I was transmitted, pinioned and loaded with irons, to London, there to await a ship to take me to Botany Bay.*

In fact, he was sent to Van Dieman's Land. He was sixty years old, and now his family were out there, all felons.

Thanks to Tony Satchell, in an interesting book linked to the heritage industry today in Australia called *For Better or Worse*, we have a lively account of the family of Dunhills. Snowden's wife, Sarah, who was also sixty when she was sentenced to seven years' transportation in 1819, had been taken to Sydney on board the *Lord Wellington* and she had been assigned as a servant to a man in Windsor. She managed to attain a certification to give her freedom and so she went to Hobart to find her family. She died in 1838 at Richmond. The Dunhill family were mostly convicted of felonies, and as Tony Satchell points out, only one child, Elizabeth, escaped transportation.

Tony Satchell's book not only gives profiles of the Dunhills taken from documents, but it also offers a portrait line drawing of both Snowden and Sarah. Snowden, who thought he looked like Sir Walter Scott, looks out at the reader with a cheery face, well-fed and quite healthy: not at all what we think of as the face of a transported convict. Snowden Dunhill died in the same year as his wife, and he is buried on the Isle of the Dead, an island which may be seen from one end of the penitentiary site, and on this place the convicts from the site were buried.

Snowden had in fact managed to be given a position of some responsibility at Port Arthur, being appointed sub-overseer. But as usual with him, he sank again after petty offences. His story shows very clearly how it was possible for a convict to return to civil life as a free citizen, as long as he played along with the system and could keep his good health. The life was hard and the temptations many, but a large number of people came home with that ticket of leave.

As for the Dunhills, they illustrate the popular belief that crime runs in families, and that it takes a lot of shifting from its place in the mindset once the people are inured to the life of crime.

Chapter 8

CRIMINAL LUNATICS

The context
What defines an 'unsound mind?' How may a court of law decide on this, in the legal process? How far is expert testimony reliable?

Throughout British history and the course of the legal system, notions of what constitutes insanity have been problematic. When it comes to assessing whether or not a criminal act is carried out while the offender is in a permanent state of insanity or not, the pitfalls in legal argument are many and complex. Everything depends on the presence of a defect of reason. The important test question is: 'Would he have committed the crime if a policeman had been standing at his elbow?'

The important landmark in this context was what has become known as the M'Naghten Rules. This refers to the 1843 case of Daniel M'Naghten who, while he thought he was murdering Sir Robert Peel, actually killed another person. The defence was shaped after a list of questions was put before a bench of judges, and the result was that there was a set of rules which would, in theory, define whether or not a criminal act was done by a person who was arguably insane.

For many centuries, as the common law and its commentators and theorists sought to explain what insanity was, some kind of groundwork was done and a distinction between what was called 'mental insufficiency' and 'mental perversity' was drawn. Homer Crotty explains the difference: 'The first term comprehends those whom the law knows as idiots, and the second those whom the law knows as lunatics. In the first group there is a lack of something in the mental make-up, whereas in the second there is a disorder of the mind which the subject possesses'.

To the modern mind, the term 'idiot' is offensive to sensibilities. But in times past, all kinds of terms were used, and they had specific meanings. Homer Crotty extracts relevant material from early legal texts:

> *One of the most striking things about the early law is the number and variety of terms used to describe the mentally abnormal. These terms are in Latin, Law French and English, and may be divided into two classes: those denoting the idiot, and those denoting the lunatic. Those denoting the idiot are apparently used as equivalents for the terms which we today [1924] apply to the lower grades of mental defectives, and would therefore include the idiot and the imbecile.*

It is hard to swallow today, but those terms were used for centuries and they had specific meanings in the law and in medicine.

In the sixteenth century, one of the great legal writers relating to English common law was Anthony Fitzherbert, and he made, in *La Novelle Natura Brevium* (1534), a distinction between two widely used terms:

> *And he who shall be said to be a Sot and Idiot from his birth is such a person who cannot accompt or number a twenty-pence, nor can tell who was his father or mother, or how old he is … so as it may appear that he hath no understanding of Reason what shall be for his profit and what for his loss …*

When the modern researcher looks into an ancestor who may have been classified in a certain way and seen as insane, any one of a cluster of such terms may be used.

The great expansion of mental asylums through the nineteenth century reflects the ways in which various conceptions of insanity were applied and agreed on. By the outbreak of the First World War in 1914, the county of Surrey alone had fourteen asylums, and in terms of criminal insanity, it is interesting to note that one of these was for epileptics. There had been cases in Victorian times in which epileptic conditions were on the borderline when it came to pleas of insanity in court, and it was after a Lincolnshire case in which a blacksmith had killed a police officer that matters changed regarding epileptic conditions and criminal offences.

The madness of George III in the early nineteenth century had highlighted the treatment of the insane, and a division had developed between those medical people who believed in gentle regimes with exercise and close supervision, and others who still saw harsh physical treatments such as cold baths and restraints as curative.

From the 1860s in particular, the massive asylums gradually inculcated a certain set of attitudes and related therapies. These were largely based on fresh air and exercise, dialogues, sociability and good, nutritious food. Gardening was considered to be especially beneficial. There were specialist institutions, such as the one already mentioned for epileptics, but there was also an Idiot Asylum for children. It was realised that children should be kept apart from adult lunatics.

From the mid twentieth century, the nomenclature changed, as there were advances in the understanding of mental illness. By the Criminal Justice Act of 1948 there was a particular paragraph which clarified this:

62. Discontinuance of terms 'criminal lunatic' and 'criminal lunatic asylum.'
(1) Asylums and places appointed under section 1 of the Criminal Lunatic Asylums Act, 1860, shall be called and are in this Act referred to as "Broadmoor institutions;" and accordingly for references to criminal lunatic asylums (by whatever name called) in any enactment there shall be substituted references to Broadmoor institutions.'

DESCRIPTION
OF
THE RETREAT,
AN INSTITUTION NEAR YORK

For Insane Persons

OF THE

SOCIETY OF FRIENDS.

CONTAINING AN ACCOUNT OF ITS

ORIGIN AND PROGRESS,

The Modes of Treatment,

AND

A STATEMENT OF CASES.

By SAMUEL TUKE.

With an Elevation and Plans of the Building.

This was an early instance of the more enlightened treatment of the insane. (From Samuel Tuke, Description of the Retreat *1813)*

'Broadmoor' thus became a generic term for asylums.

The relevant point here with reference to family history is that asylums provided alternatives to prisons in some cases at law, when the question of the felon's sanity was mooted. Thus the variety of institutions that catered for the mentally ill will always be a relevant research topic when prisons come to mind. Sometimes, if wealth and facilities for personal care were available, a prison sentence or a life inside asylum walls might be avoided. Such was the case with Mary, the sister of the writer Charles Lamb (1775–1834), who murdered their mother in a fit of violent insanity. Of course, her story and those like it would have faded away into obscurity. For ordinary folk, the asylum was waiting after such a crime.

It is useful, then, if an ancestor committed a serious crime, and this was an offence against the person or against property, to think in terms of destinations, in this sense: the crime is arguably one done while insane; the legal process goes from magistrate's court or quarter sessions to assizes; the possible destinations are: prison, asylum, the noose, transportation.

The documentation will be considerable in many cases.

Broadmoor Prison and Hospital

It was recognised that for a number of categories of mental illness, there was a need for special custody. From this emerged the now iconic Broadmoor – a word which has become something that denotes extreme criminal mental illness and psychopathic threat.

Broadmoor was built across 290 acres of land in Berkshire after the Criminal Lunatics Act of 1860, which planned better care and custody of criminal lunatics. Ultimately, we could trace the sources of the attitudes behind this to the trial of James Hadfield, who had tried to murder George III back in 1800 and who had been saved the noose on the grounds of insanity. But of course, taking a wider view, it may be easily adduced today that many other social factors were at work in creating those offenders who became labelled 'criminal lunatics'. More recent research and biography has shown that very creative people who were guilty of criminal offences were held there, as they needed special treatment and observation. Basically, they required something other than being kept in a local gaol or in a convict prison.

Broadmoor, designed by Joshua Jebb, opened in 1863 with ninety-five female patients. Soon after that males were admitted, and by late 1865 there were 500 patients held there, of which 200 were women.

The advances were significant. In 1832, the Chairman of the Prison Discipline Society gave evidence to a Select Committee on Secondary

Punishments and he referred to the treatment of lunatics in criminal prisons. The Chairman reported:

It is not generally known, but at Exeter prison there is one lunatic who has been confined for 22 years, another 16 years and two for 12 years. In Wiltshire one above 10 years; in Pembroke 22 years and Anglesey for 13 years.

The available records

As a useful general search, Ancestry.co.uk has Lunacy Registers and Warrants for 1820–1912. Among these are found celebrities of true crime literature such as Roderick McLean (see below) and Jack the Ripper suspect Aaron Kosminski.

At The National Archives the main resources are for administration records rather than for inmates, and the online note tells the reader:

Records of lunatic asylums are not held in any one place and often not all of their records have survived. Many records of asylums, prisons and houses of correction are kept in local archives …

For the larger picture, therefore, at The National Archives will be found:

- *Patients' admission registers for 1846–1912*. These were generated by the Lunacy Commission and Board of Control.
- *Criminal Lunacy warrant and entry books for 1882–1898*. These refer to those who were certified at trial as criminal lunatics. Sometimes, the certification was done after imprisonment.
- *Criminal Lunatic asylum registers for 1800–1843*. These are searchable at Ancestry.co.uk for a subscription fee.
- *Correspondence with Poor Law unions and other local authorities*. These are listed by county, so a first check here would lead to the right county record office database.

For Broadmoor, The National Archives has introductory information, and this leads to the Berkshire Record Office. At Berkshire there are:

- General records – for 1861–2002
- Finance records – for 1867–1973
- Estates – for 1864–1988
- Staff – for 1863–1990
- Clinical and patients – for 1863–1943

Annual return: Insane persons. A return showing some information, the inmates with severe mental illness who were admitted to a home for special care. (East Riding Archives)

There have been several publications on Broadmoor, and some of these give accounts of the prisoners. The regime was notably innovative and gentle, with a whole series of secondary therapies (although those words would not have been used in late Victorian times). In particular, the Victorians' belief in art, gardening and creative hobbies was placed highly in the regime. Simon Winchester's book, *The Surgeon of Crowthorne* (1999), gives a very informative account of Broadmoor in this period.

Case study: the would-be Queen killers

In March 1882, Queen Victoria went into London to hold a 'Drawing room' social event at Buckingham Palace. After that she and Princess Beatrice went back to Windsor on Thursday afternoon (2 March) by train from Paddington. Arriving at Windsor at almost 5.30pm, Victoria crossed the platform to walk to her waiting carriage. She and Beatrice stepped inside and as the outrider moved, so did the carriage, but at that moment, as cheers were raised all around, a young man approached with a gun in his hand and fired at the carriage.

This was Roderick Maclean, and luckily he was a poor shot. The driver moved off smartly and the gunman was overhauled, grabbed by the intrepid Superintendent Hayes of Windsor Police. With him was Inspector Fraser of the Metropolitan Police, an officer assigned to the

Royal Household. Shabby Maclean, from Victoria Cottages in Windsor, was set about by the public as well, including two Eton scholars who attacked him with an umbrella. When the young man was securely held, he said, 'Don't hurt me, I did it through starvation ...' He had fired two ball cartridges from his German pistol. The bullet meant for the queen missed the carriage and hit a truck beyond.

Maclean went to trial in Reading and was declared insane. He was a pathetic figure, having just a few coppers on his person when searched, and it was reported than he lived 'an idle life in beggarly poverty'. He was later given a state trial and found guilty of what was of course a capital offence. However, he was found not guilty on the grounds of insanity. The charge was 'traitorously and maliciously compassing the death of her Majesty the Queen and with having on March 2 discharged a pistol loaded with powder and bullet at Her Majesty'. One report at the time said, 'The prisoner took his place calmly ... During the time he had been in prison his clothes had got shabbier than when he was arrested ...'

Maclean was, of course, in an asylum for the course of his natural life. *The Penny Illustrated Paper* reported on the closing moments of the trial:

> *On being called upon to plead, the prisoner said, 'Not guilty my Lord'. The case was the outlined by the Attorney General, who called the witnesses, ... Mr Montague Williams called witnesses who gave clear proofs of Maclean's insanity. The jury retired at twenty minutes to five and after five minutes' deliberation, returned into court and delivered a verdict of Not Guilty on the grounds of insanity. The Lord Chief Justice ordered the prisoner to be detained under Her Majesty's Pleasure.*

Queen Victoria and various members of her family tended to travel without much fear of attack. Often they rode in an open carriage and only one or two staff members of the Royal Household would be around. Illustrations in contemporary books and periodicals show the open-topped carriages of royalty, often without much awareness of security. The picture from *The Illustrated London News* showing Maclean's attack makes it clear that there was a horseman in front of the carriage, but no escort to the side who might have blocked the would-be assassin's view and his shot, of course. Partly this was because of the certainty that Victoria, centre of the vast British Empire, was adored by all. Men and women were giving their lives across the world for that ideal, serving her wherever the map was painted red.

However, she was clearly a target. Not only had there previously been an intruder into her rooms at Buckingham Palace, but in the year of her wedding to Prince Albert, 1840, there had also been a much more threatening attack. This was by a teenage pot-boy who was out of work. He was in a secret society, some said, and may well have been a stooge in a wider plot. It was a time of active radical violence, and there were some factions in society who wanted the queen dead.

Edward Oxford took advantage of the couple taking an evening ride in an open carriage along Constitution Hill. He had been standing in Green Park and came forward with a gun in his hand and fired it at her majesty. Prince Albert saved the queen's life, as he put his hand behind her head and pushed it forward. He had seen the assassin come to them and saw what was going to happen.

A pamphlet at the time reported that the young man was soon captured, but not before he fired a second shot from another pistol, which missed the target. The report says:

The prince directed the carriage to proceed as if nothing had happened. The villain who made this diabolical attempt was seized by a number of persons who rushed towards him, and on the arrival of the police he was taken to Queen's Square office.

Oxford was from Birmingham and he had been working as a pot boy at a tavern called the Hog in the Pound on the Marylebone Road. When his room in West Street was searched there were some sinister revelations: they found a black crepe cap and powder flask, along with pistols. One report on the incident said, 'the true moral courage of our beloved sovereign had ruled supreme.'

In 1842, John Francis tried to take the queen's life and this time two bullets were fired at her. He was convicted of using gunpowder and other destructive material and sentenced to death. But Francis had his sentence commuted to life imprisonment. Amazingly, Victoria was still moving around in a brash and fearless way when, just two days after Francis's attempt on her life, a man called John William Bean fired a loaded pistol at her. Again she survived, and public opinion was a mix of deep concern and astonishment that nothing more active was being done to protect her. Bean was called a 'hunchback miscreant' by *The Illustrated London News* reporter. The police reacted to this by rounding up all the deformed young men they could come across. Bean escaped from custody; the two constables in charge of him were sacked. Victoria's brazen facing of danger and refusal to break routine could only increase the love and respect her people had for her. As she went to the opera shortly after the 1842 attacks, as she entered her box there was a loud

Attempt on the Life of Queen Victoria: poster describing the attempted assassination by Edward Oxford. (Author)

applause and the performance had to stop as there was a 'demonstration of the liveliest joy' from the crowd.

Oxford is the most interesting case in some ways. He went to Broadmoor as being criminally insane, rather than being hanged, and in 1867 there was discussion of him at the highest level, and the Home

Secretary, Gathorne Hardy, wrote to Broadmoor to request a report on Oxford's condition. If the prisoner was classified as being sane and then freed, he could have carried on life in England. But the government wanted him out of the country, and he went to Melbourne with a new name: John Freeman. In late 1867, Oxford wrote, while in Broadmoor, 'In leaving England forever I do what is certainly the best'.

It would still take a very long time for the concept of 'diminished responsibility' in a criminal offence to be conceived and implemented as a defence. There is also much research showing that mental illness is still a factor in prison life and sentences, and that many prisoners who are in mainstream gaols should arguably be in mental health institutions. In earlier times, mental illness was a floating concept, depending on which medical condition was in question. For instance, there have been cases in which sufferers from epilepsy have been sentenced to hang, only to be saved by medical testimony. (See my book *Lincolnshire Murders*, listed in the Bibliography.)

Chapter Nine

SECONDARY RECORDS

Young offenders

As will surely have become obvious in the foregoing accounts of the court system through the centuries since the arrival of the assizes and the development of the local bench for magistrates' courts, children and young adults were merely part of the overall regime when it came to the process of law and prison sentences. For centuries, children were thrown in among adult prisoners; until John Howard came along and enquired more deeply into penal conditions, very few people had given any thought to what the Victorians called 'contamination' in prisons.

Added to this is the general historical commentary of those centuries, and this shows us that children were primarily considered as workers as soon as they could perform physical tasks – at least, as far as the working and middling classes were concerned. But this is not to say that efforts were not made, at least in theory, to distinguish between adult and child offenders.

As far back as the reign of Athelstan (925–940) a law was passed which included this:

> said to him seemed and to those with whom he took counsel, that men should slay none younger than a fifteen winter's man, unless he would defend himself or flee, and would not yield, then let men force him, the greater as the less, whoever it were. And if he then will yield, let him be set in gaol, and so let him be redeemed.

But this thinking never came to much. When we move on to the Georgian period and the hundreds of capital offences, there were many executions of children, and large numbers were jailed. As usual with our penal system, for centuries before reforms and the establishment of Borstal, work was seen as the remedy for juvenile crime. Sir John Fielding, chief magistrate at Bow Street, commented that:

> *there are ... in town many hundreds of this kind of boys who might be made useful to society if they were collected together before they commenced thieves and placed either in men-of-war or the Merchants' Service.*

In the nineteenth century, for many decades the mixed population in prisons – by age, gender and all other factors – is quickly seen in the general census records. This is an extract from the 1861 census for Northallerton prison (formerly a house of correction):

Name	Age and marital status	Occupation	Place of birth or domicile
James Wilton	31 Single	Agricultural labourer	Methwold, Norfolk
Robert Johnson	14 Single	Print warehouse labourer	Liverpool
William Jones	14 Single	Shipping warehouse labourer	Liverpool

In the female wings:

Elizabeth Grady	10 Single	Pottery labourer	Scotland
Sarah Grady	40 Widowed	Washerwoman	North Sea
Mary Ann Appleton	15 Single	House servant all work	Brompton

As is usually the case, the first moves towards reforming the penal system regarding its treatment of young offenders were small-scale and experimental. Before any direct legislation, this was a trend. For instance, in 1818 there was an establishment in Warwickshire which was labelled a 'farm colony'. Writing in 1938, Geraldine Cadbury noted 'It is difficult to find the place today, but at the pretty village of Stretton-on-Dunsmore an old lady remembers that Hill Farm was originally called Asylum Farm.' Cadbury's book, *Young Offenders: Yesterday and Today* was one of the few general accounts of the subject in the first half of the twentieth century.

Twenty years after the Warwickshire experiment, the government at last made a move in this area. It established special facilities and a regime for boys who had been sentenced to transportation, at Parkhurst prison on the Isle of Wight. In 1847, at a House of Lords enquiry, the governor, Captain Hall, had this to say:

On the boy's first arrival at the prison he is placed in a probationary ward where he is kept in separate confinement for four months or more ... On leaving Parkhurst they are generally sent to the colonies ...

In 1895 the Gladstone Committee came up with the idea of the 'borstal' and the man behind this was Sir Evelyn Ruggles-Brise, who was a prison commissioner. The first institution was at Borstal, near Rochester, and came into operation by 1902. The word 'borstal' later became a generic term for such places. The 1908 Prevention of Crime Act brought together the thinking on the subject, and put forward the required regime and functions of these special prisons. Again, as had been the case with the new prisons in the 1870s, the stress was on work and discipline, with education integrated. The Act also created the notion of separate juvenile courts.

The Criminal Justice Act of 1982 abolished the borstal system and consequently there were detention centres, and later our current provision, namely Young Offenders' Institutes (YOIs).

Before these advances, Victorian Britain had *reformatories* and *industrial schools*. As a consequence of the Youthful Offenders Act of 1854 and the Industrial Schools Act of 1857, forty-eight reformatories were established by the 1860s. Estimates suggest that by the end of the century, 30,000 children were held either in industrial schools or reformatories.

Even more massive in scale is the whole business of juvenile delinquency; in 1916, the Liverpool Education Committee, appointed in a state of alarm over the number of young offenders appearing at the City Juvenile Court, reported that the punishment of whipping should be maintained. Of course, many fathers were away at war, but discipline had to be enforced, and justices were given the power to impose whipping on boys up to the age of fourteen.

Certain places had more problems with youth crime than others. Liverpool was arguably the place of the reformatory. In the nineteenth century the city had the *Clarence* reformatory school ship for boys, off New Ferry. This was a battleship that had been built in 1827. In 1884, it was burnt out in an arson attack by six of the boys. It was replaced by the *Royal William*, but that too experienced a mutiny and a burning. Boys were dispersed across the land, many to the Whitwick reformatory in Leicestershire. In 1856 it was the largest in the country, and took many delinquent boys from Liverpool.

After the Juvenile Offenders Act of 1847, young offenders could be tried at summary courts, and then in 1854, reformatories began to replace prisons as their destination. The rough, tough Liverpool lads who went to Whitwick caused such a serious riot in 1863 that eight constables were called out. One constable from Shepsted was seriously injured. That saga would be a book on its own, and any writing on Liverpool tends to have that effect: the subject expands, so great is the narrative potential of this complex yet wonderful city. It has the reputation of being a creative, bustling place, on the edge on Britain, looking across to America and Ireland. Its complexity is such that it has always had a volatile mix of races and religions in its demography. In the midst of all this, naturally there had been crime.

When the borstals came along at the end of the nineteenth century, of course there were weaknesses and problems. It was experimental. The lawyer J.B. Sandbach, who was a London Police Court magistrate, located the basic weakness:

> *The Borstal boy ... has to produce two certificates. One from the Justices to say that he has been convicted the requisite number of times, and the other a committal order from the court which dealt with him, which proves that he is far enough advanced in crime to need special treatment. So that Borstal starts with a hundred per cent bad material to work on. The wonder is not that they get so many failures but that they do not get more.*
>
> (*This Old Wig*, see Bibliography)

Records at The National Archives for materials on administration of borstals are at HO 247 and these refer to the Borstal Association After Care Association, covering the years 1905–1977. These are reports, registers and files. Borstals are also covered at HO45 for the years 1839–1879 and these are listed with dozens of other topics from that period.

After that the sources are regional, and a typical example is at Liverpool where, as mentioned earlier in this section, there was a high demand and provision for and in answer to juvenile detention. The records of the Liverpool Catholic Reformatory Association are held at the Liverpool Record Office. But these are such items as minute books, journals, cash books and subscription books. These were assembled and maintained after the 1854 Act referred to in this section. As the Liverpool website says:

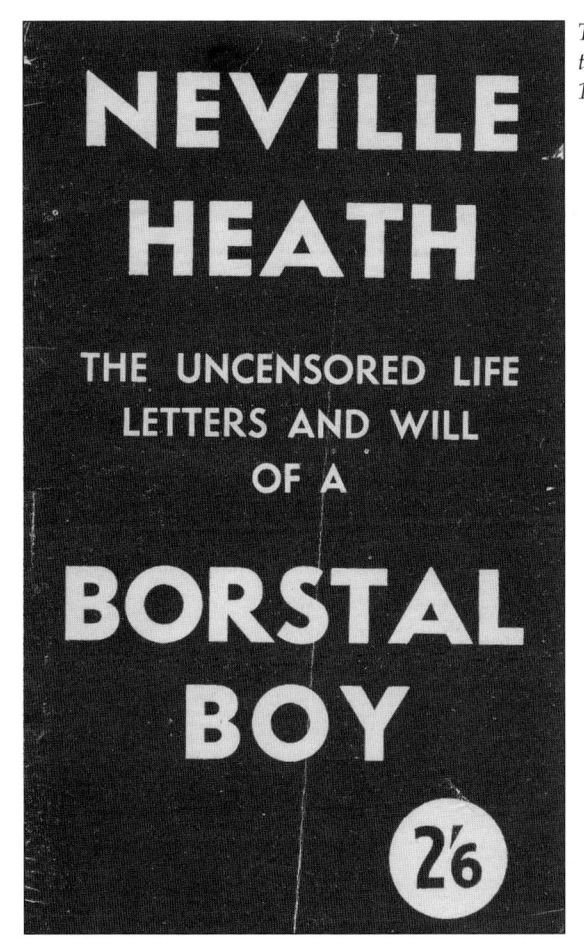

The cover of a memoir by the notorious Neville Heath, 1946. (Author)

> Under the terms of the Act a voluntary institution could on application to the Home Office be inspected and if found satisfactory, be certified ...

Wider Sources

In the demanding and enthralling process of researching the life and crimes of ancestors, one thing soon becomes clear: sources are hard to find and are often piecemeal. One tends to find that there are missing stretches and gaps. There is basic information in the mainstream documentation, with the prison calendars and returns at the centre, and then the research becomes more difficult and the information more elusive.

It is with this mind that the experience of other historians and researchers becomes invaluable. The internet will throw up any number of brief references to a particular criminal, in all kinds of contexts, and these have to be listed and assembled. The sources from more disparate and distant sources gradually become important. These secondary sources may be listed in this way:

- Reports and enquiries
- Newspaper reports
- Biographies and memoirs
- Almanacs and local publications
- Journals and diaries
- National magazines: *The Annual Register/The Gentleman's Magazine*

In their own specific ways, all of these have the potential to build on the basic knowledge given in prison documents. Sometimes, the researcher will never extract much more than:

> *William Finch, gardener, pleaded guilty of stealing a saddle worth 3d, a bridle worth 6d and a saddlecloth worth 2d.*

Or even:

> *Nicholas Powell and William Powell, husbandmen, to be kept in gaol until they pay their fine of 10s and fees of 6s 9d.*

Other sources may present a narrative. For instance, researching a Lincolnshire orphan, from the 1870s–1880s, this sequence of records was gathered:

- The calendar of prisoners: list of a dozen details, relating to work and education etc.
- Then the reference to the girl in a journal
- Finally this, from a home for many desperate, orphaned or impoverished girls: 'Brought to the Home by the matron of the city prison, Oct 21st 1874'.

In other words, sometimes we have to move laterally to give more substance to a biographical outline.

At the heart of the research, as a first step, the newspaper archive is hard to beat. This would be the sequence of enquiries in a typical search of a criminal life in Victorian Britain:

1. What do I know already?
He was called Joseph Ralph and he was in gaol at Lincoln in the 1850s

2. First search?
The online newspapers for the 1850s, search term 'Lincoln assizes.'

His name is given in short reports in *The Times* or in regional newspaper reports (*Times Digital Archive/ British Newspapers Online*). The sweep of reports includes brief trial material but then this: 'A prisoner named Joseph Ralph, 30 years of age, who was sentenced to 20 years transportation by Sir James Parke, at the Lincoln Assizes on Monday the 24th., escaped from Lincoln Castle on Thursday last …'

3. What have I learned that I can use to find more?
In the report there are these facts: his offence was burglary in 1836; he had been transferred from Lincoln to Millbank; he came from York and he had a mole under his left eye.

4. Does the narrative end locally or does it extend further?
Most often, a crime of burglary or theft will consist of the prison record and a brief newspaper report. But John Ralph escaped. He had, it turns out, been held in prisons at Leeds, Lincoln and Millbank and was destined to be transported. *The Nottingham Journal* reported the prison escape in more detail, and a week later, another paper noted that the Lincoln prison governor had been sacked.

As a general guide, the approach is to check out every cross-reference given from the first brief report. Clearly, after the 1870s there is much more information in the registers and returns so there is more to follow up.

Incidents and reports shine a light
One very substantial resource for prison records is the collection of parliamentary papers. For prison history and information, the reports from the Commissioner, inspector of prisons and others are remarkably useful. A typical volume is the volume of reports from Holloway Sanatorium for 1896. This includes: architectural plans; boarders; suicides; post mortems; institution for idiots and state institutions, including Broadmoor. And this just one of many. The nature of these bound reports is related to the Houses of Commons and Lords; the printed reports of enquiries, from all areas of government, include prisons, asylums and all other related establishments. The National Archives has access to a digitised set online, as do readers of the Wellcome Library who can access this material at home. The papers are arranged according to the parliamentary year. For instance, for a decade in the mid-Victorian years, the volumes include reports and enquiries on such topics as convict

prisons, transportation, local gaols and such specific topics as conditions, education or health.

A good place to start is at the Bodleian Library in Oxford. If a researcher wants to read the actual papers in volumes, then the Bodleian keeps a full set. Other university libraries may well have this too. The University of Hull, for instance, has a similar stock. (See https://libguides.bodleian.ox.ac.uk/parliament/1800-2000)

In terms of prison history, the foundation of all good source material lies in the fact that it is when prison regimes go wrong that they generate a mass of documentation and reports. In the modern age, if there is a riot or a mutiny inside the walls, the paper trail will be voluminous and of course there will be press and internet coverage in some depth.

Historically, an accessible way to understand this, and to see how names crop up and prisoners become visible from the mass of the prison population, is in state papers. The following is an account of one state trial: *The Trial of John Huggins, Warden of the Fleet Prison, for the murder of Edward Arne* (1729).

Huggins bought the wardenship of the Fleet for the huge sum of £5,000 for himself and his son. Of course he then had to get the investment back by any means possible. The Fleet was at that time mainly a debtors' prison, and we know what it was like because the great reformer John Howard reported on it. At that time, debtors' prisons had two sides: Common and the Masters. On the latter side lived those who could afford to rent their accommodation, but the Common side, as Howard describes, was horrendous:

> *The apartments for the Common-side debtors are only part of the right wing ... Besides the cellar there are four floors. On each floor is a room about twenty four or five feet square, with a fire-place; and on the sides seven closets or cabins to sleep in. Such of the prisoners who swear in court or before a commissioner that they cannot subsist without charity, have the donations which are sent to the prison, and the begging box and grate.'*

The grate was the street-level aperture from which they could beg passers-by for alms or even just water. But their situation would have normally been like that of the anonymous writer to the *Gentleman's Magazine*, were it not for the fact that John Huggins and his gang of assistants were sadists. At the basis of the sentence was the table of fees for the gaolers: these included fees for the chaplain, the porter, the chamberlain, the turnkey, and added to that were fees for 'liberty of the house and irons when first coming in' and a dismission fee. The total cost of all these fees was supposed to be under £2, but in fact £3 5s was the sum taken, as increments were applied.

Huggins decided, as he aged, that he would sell his position to a certain Thomas Bambridge, his deputy, along with another scoundrel called Dougal Cuthbert. A barbaric and murderous regime was to follow, and the scandal broke not long after Bambridge took control. At the centre of the affair was the death of a prisoner, Edward Arne, who had been committed to a horrible den called the Strongroom where he starved and suffered infections and diseases so extreme that he lost his wits before dying a miserable death inside the walls. At the trial, the Strongroom was described by a witness called Bigrave:

Solicitor-General:	What do you know of the building the strong room?
Bigrave:	When I came there there was a stable which was converted into a strong room …
Solicitor-General:	What sort of a place is it?
Bigrave:	It is arched like a wine vault, built of brick and mortar.
Solicitor-General:	What are the dimensions?
Bigrave:	It is eight feet wide and eleven feet long.
Solicitor-General:	How near was the dung-hill to it?
Bigrave:	The dunghill was as nigh as to the other part of the court.

Another witness called Bishop said, referring to Arne:

When he was brought in he was in good condition of health and in his senses … being put in the strong room in the Fleet would have killed anybody, and that forwarded Arne's death.

Poor Arne's last days were pitiable. A turnkey called Farringdon gave the most touching account of the man's death:

he grew somewhat disordered and from the time he was put in the strong room he altered every day, grew hoarse, and at last could not speak, and he grew weaker and weaker every day; about the beginning of October he lost his voice, he then grew delirious, and ripped open his bed, and crept into the feathers, and one day he came to chapel with excrement and feathers sticking to him like a magpie, being forced to ease nature in that place … After that I saw the prisoner at the bar looking into the strong room, the door being open, and Arne was lying in the bed ripped open …

The trial was widely reported and brought into the public eye the lamentable state of the debtors in His Majesty's prisons. The story of Huggins and Bambridge came out in full as witnesses were examined. Huggins had left Bambridge to take over, before actually selling him the office of warden, but Huggins had stayed at home, miles out of London, and had only been to the Fleet twice over a period of nine months. He had left the prison in the control of a cruel, heartless monster who only wanted the profit, and was only too happy to see the prisoners die if they could not pay his fees.

The trial was reported in detail, and the text of the state trial used a parliamentary report and enquiry: *A Report from the Committee of the House of Commons appointed to Inquire into the state of the Gaols of this Kingdom, so far as Relates to the cruel Usage of Prisoners* dated 20 March 1729. In the process of the enquiry, several prisoners are named and described, such as 'Jacob Mendez Solas, a Portuguese, was, as far as it appeared to the Committee, one of the first prisoners for debt that ever was loaded with irons in the Fleet'. Then, the text of the trial is given, and other prisoners speak, as in this exchange, in which Thomas Farrington is an ex-prisoner:

Attorney-General:	Did you know Edward Arne?
Farringdon:	I did ...
Attorney-General:	What state of heath was he in?
Farringdon:	When he came into the Fleet prison he was in a good state of health, and free from any sort of deliriousness, and I never saw him do anything amiss to man, woman or child.

Basically, in the records of any extraordinary events there will be named prisoners and staff.

Fortunately, the parliamentary papers and state trials are mostly online and some are actually in print, in book form. See the Bibliography for a reference to this.

Other reports may be slender, and the time-consuming element in this is that a listing of documents online will usually be only a brief description, such as this from the West Yorkshire Archives, under 'Wakefield Prison Records': 'C118/1 Director's minute book: 1907–1912 It records visits almost every month to inspect the prison, to hear prisoners' applications etc.'

This is the most common obstacle. The question has to be asked, when deciding what to order and check out, is this likely to have prisoners' names recorded? Unless the researcher is happy to spend every hour

> NOTES
>
> ON A VISIT MADE TO SOME OF
>
> THE PRISONS
>
> IN
>
> Scotland
>
> AND
>
> The North of England,
>
> IN COMPANY WITH
>
> ELIZABETH FRY;
>
> WITH SOME GENERAL OBSERVATIONS ON THE SUBJECT OF PRISON DISCIPLINE.
>
> By JOSEPH JOHN GURNEY.
>
> SECOND EDITION.
>
> LONDON:
> PRINTED FOR
> ARCHIBALD CONSTABLE AND CO., EDINBURGH;
> LONGMAN, HURST, REES, ORME, AND BROWN,
> JOHN AND ARTHUR ARCH,
> AND HURST, ROBINSON, AND COMPANY, LONDON.
>
> 1819.

Joseph Gurney was one of many Quakers who visited the prisons. This, the title page of Notes on a Visit to Some of the prisons in Scotland and the North of England. *(Constable, 1819)*

available in looking through these types of sources, a selection has to be made.

Memoirs

Throughout history, people working in the criminal justice system and offenders who have served time in that system have had their stories to tell. These memoirs include prison experience, and if a particular convict has served time in a prison during the time-period of an ancestor, then there are possibilities for useful information, as will be seen in the next section with the story of Michael Davitt.

The memoirs may be written by barristers, judges, police officers, prison staff and of course, by ex-inmates. These, together with printed volumes of court records (only of sensational and serious cases) present the possibility that blanks may be filled in, biographically and of course also in terms of our understanding of the process of conviction and sentence trajectory. In the modern prison system, a prisoner will be allotted an officer to work with him or her on a project called 'sentence planning'. In the past we did not have this, but we do have the voluminous records, at least in some cases, tracking the course of a person's prison history. If this material can be placed alongside something relevant in a memoir, then the biography really becomes substantial.

What tends to happen in the average memoir by a barrister, for instance, is that the names in the accounts of all the cases will only be those whose names and stories are already in newspaper reports. But often, a memoir or a biography of a lawyer will include something additional to the known, printed narrative.

In the age in which virtually anyone with a radical thought or who might have joined a club or society lived in fear of arrest – the late Regency – memoirs tend to have accounts of a number of prisons. These provide a rich source of information on gaols of the period in which the ancestor would have been detained. One of the most fertile for sources in these years is Samuel Bamford's *Passages in the Life of a Radical*, which he started writing in 1839 and was printed in 1844. Bamford, a Lancashire man, experienced several prisons during his life of political agitation, including 'the new bailey', a dungeon at Manchester, and Lincoln, where he witnessed a hanging.

Biographies

As with memoirs, biographies have their place. They are often overlooked in research into criminal lives, but in fact the type of biography that takes in social history and the context of crime at a certain time is rich in sources. Many are out of print, and so they are best for the kind of research undertaken in a full day at a major library. Much pre-1835 material has been digitised at the Hathi Trust, Google Books and the Internet Archive.

I would recommend having a reader's ticket at a university library. Many of these libraries have numerous volumes of biography, and also have parliamentary papers. My own writing after research has been enriched by the use of these categories in particular: memoirs of barristers, detectives, prison governors and of course, prisoners themselves, and also the occasional police officer's memoirs or a biography of a particular officer.

One of the most useful sources in this category is the book dealing with a group biography, such as the volumes written by Donald Thomas, who concentrates on the 1940s and 1950s. His accounts of crimes in those years include explanations of topics such as prison conditions, alleged bribery, the nature of particular offences, and the court processes of the time.

Equally, further back in time, the Regency and Victorian periods are well served. Barristers and judges became marketable subjects for biography as far as publishers were concerned. The 'ordinaries' (gaolers) of Newgate saw that there was money to be made in telling tales of their charges to publishers, and so the chronicles of crime began to provide biography as a genre within that area of print.

An example is needed, and for anyone with an ancestor convicted of white-collar crime in the late Victorian to Edwardian times, George Bidwell's autobiography, *Forging his Chains* is essential. Published in 1888, this volume explains in detail not only the particulars of a fraud and what it entailed, but also prison life in a convict prison, along with the process of a major trial at the Old Bailey.

For twentieth-century biography, what is most helpful to researchers is the special genre of true crime writing by prison officers and lawyers, as they usually have memories of prisons and prisoners, and they present perspectives on criminals in specific categories of offence.

Case study: a Fenian memoir
In my book *Foul Deeds and Suspicious Deaths in Doncaster* (2010), I recalled the story of Thomas Slack, who in 1867 murdered his wife, Hannah. He was found guilty and sentenced to twenty years of penal servitude. That would mean that he would go to a convict prison, and a researcher would look for him in one of the southern prisons, either on the Isle of Wight or maybe Dartmoor. He could most likely have been traced on the registers there, but anyone doing a search for possible secondary sources, looking for 'Dartmoor 1860–1880' could easily find memoirs, and one of them was by the Irish republican, Michael Davitt.

I originally wrote up the story for the website 'Doncaster History' (see Bibliography) as 'Captain Slack's Undoing'. At the time, writing Slack's story for the book, it seemed that there were no more records pertaining to him. It was simply one more nasty murder story from Yorkshire. But then a memoir brought a surprise.

Davitt (1846–1906) was an Irish republican, very much involved with the land laws and the struggle against the English landlords, who also became mixed up in the mainland bombing campaigns in Britain, and was arrested in London, waiting for some arms to be delivered; his sentence was fifteen years' penal servitude. He served time in Millbank, and then at Dartmoor. In 1877 he acquired a ticket of leave. While in prison he was questioned by a board of enquiry. The questions posed tell us a great deal about prison life in a convict prison at the time.

In Dartmoor, Davitt met Slack, and he wrote about him as the type of prisoner who always lived with the optimism of a possible parole and freedom. This provides a perfect example of how, by sheer serendipity, the life of a convict ancestor may be studied as the material goes beyond the bare prison records to a longer reference in a memoir.

Slack had completed seven years of his sentence and was in Dartmoor when Davitt arrived, and they sat and talked. Slack told him that after a year in gaol his brother wrote to him advising hope and patience. Then six years passed. Davitt and Slack had this conversation:

'And have you not heard from your brother these six years?' I asked, after listening to his story of drink, murder and repentance.

'Oh no' he replied, 'Did not he say I need not expect to have a letter again until he could send a good one? I am expecting one now, every day, and I think that as I have served seven years the Secretary of State will send me my release, coming on Christmas.'

Slack was then taken to another prison and Davitt did not see him for another five years; then he was brought back from Portsmouth and Davitt asked the same question, and Slack replied, 'As I have done twelve years now without a report, I am certain the Secretary of State will soon discharge me.' Davitt concluded that if the 'wretch' was ever told of his brother's conduct, he would have been 'released by death' before he had served half his term.

As for Davitt, after winning his freedom he worked in socialist and nationalist causes, and even met and interviewed Leo Tolstoy. His death was ironically everyday; he died of sepsis after a tooth extraction caused an infection.

Chapter Ten

CONTEMPORARY SOURCES IN PRINT/ONLINE

The Old Bailey sessions papers

The Old Bailey was the name given to the Central Criminal Court. It began in 1539 when the Court of Aldermen planned to establish a special court in their area; their sessions house was the centre for court functions covering London, Middlesex and some parts of the Home Counties. A sessions house was built after the Great Fire of 1666 and lasted until 1774. Then what followed was a new sessions house; Mark Herber, writing about legal London, notes, 'Sweet-smelling herbs were strewn around the courts and carried in bouquets to counter the unpleasant odours from Newgate Gaol next door.'

The building we know today dates from 1902, but since 2017 there have been major changes in operation and staff. However, the name 'Old Bailey' will always resonate through the annals of crime in Britain. It has seeped into popular culture in so many ways that the name suggests the most important, high-status trials, and that has always been the case.

It is worth noting here that assize courts ceased in 1971, and were succeeded by Crown Courts. The Old Bailey thus became a Crown Court then.

A rounded comprehension of a criminal offence and its consequences involves being clear about the contemporary context and the nature of the criminal justice system at the time the ancestor is convicted. Watching a programme on the BBC series *Who Do You Think You Are?* includes the realisation that a search into the past entails a string of various criminological experts to guide the celebrity down the highways to the past which lead through archives. Most of us cannot afford to pay all the experts. In spite of the plethora of genealogy magazines and websites, there is still one problematical hurdle in the way: the past.

Old Bailey Sessions House. A drawing of the famous Old Bailey. The trial reports from here are now available online (see Bibliography). (Author)

The writer Joseph Brodsky once wrote, in his book of essays, *Less Than One*: 'As failures go, attempting to recall the past is like trying to grasp the meaning of existence. Both make one feel like a baby clutching at a basketball: one's palms keep sliding off.' But of all the criminal records available online, this resource is arguably the one which offers most in terms of the real 'feel' for the past. The records have transcripts, and so as we read we hear the voices of the people in court, as they spoke in life.

A significant instance of this is the trial of Dr Johnson's literary friend, Dr Baretti. He was tried for murder at the Old Bailey, and Johnson (with others) was called to testify. Johnson said:

I believe I began to be acquainted with Mr Baretti about the years 53 or 54. I have been intimate with him. He is a man of literature, a very studious man, a man of great diligence. He gets his living by study. I have no reason to think he was ever disordered by liquor in his life. A man that I never knew to be otherwise than peaceable, and a man that I take to be rather timorous.

The records are not prison records, but they present trials of thousands of offenders from the late seventeenth to the early twentieth century, and so the records form an important part of your ancestor's criminal life. They are easy to use, with a straightforward search box, and even from a surname only, details soon are able to be accessed.

The London Prison records and the Tower

London has always been teeming with prisons. Mention has already been made of the main debtors' prisons, the Fleet and the Marshalsea, but there are – and were – many others. To help us through the maze of the records, there is the material provided by the London Metropolitan Archives, and they have issued *Information Leaflet number 19 Prison Records* to explain the records and the gaols. The leaflet is online, and links to the City of London mainstream resource, www.londonlives.org, where most prison records may be explained and listed.

As well as Newgate and the later convict prisons, London had several smaller gaols. These comprise, in the City of London: houses of correction at Westminster, Cold Bath Fields, Whitecross Street, Ludgate, King's Bench, Fleet, Marshalsea, Clerkenwell, Bridewell, Holloway, and Wandsworth, along with the compters at Wood Street, Poultry, Giltspur Street and Southwark. The references for the records of prisoners are all on the information sheet, but here are the principal ones:

- Calendars of Prisoners 1796–1797, 1819, 1828 at CLA/035/01/001-003
- Calendars of Middlesex Prisoners after trial 1711–1774 at MJ/CP/P/005-584
- Calendars of Prisoners (printed) 1820–1822, 1830–1853 at OB/C/P
- Receipt books for felons' goods 1857–1868 at CLA/035/02/006-017
- Schedules of felons' goods 1849–1870 at CLA/040/03/001-038
- Inquests into deaths of prisoners 1783–1839 at CLA/041/P1/001-018

There is a mass of material relating to the conditions of these prisons and about the management of them. However, some other records do concern the prisoners, such as some calendars of indictments. Records for Holloway, Wandsworth and Wormwood Scrubs are at the London Metropolitan Archives. For transportation research, Millbank records are a sensible starting-point. Millbank was the first national penitentiary, established in 1821

The *penitentiary* idea was developed in the years of the Enlightenment, being based on the notion of a large establishment which was designed in such a way that work, religious observance and efficient supervision could all progress in a controlled community. It emerged after the American War of Independence ended in 1783. From its first inception, the concept was large-scale.

As for the records of the Tower of London, these are held at a number of sites, but the main material is held at the Royal Armouries Library at the Tower itself. The National Archives have the Constable's Office records for 1610–1941 at reference WO94. Other records which would encompass prisoners are: the expenses of prisoners for 1615–16, held at the Surrey History Centre, reference 1087/1/5, and the papers of the 1st Duke of Westminster, Constable of the Tower. These are at the University of Southampton Library at reference MS 3349.

Some printed works have ample information on the political prisoners there; for the twentieth century, see John J. Eddleston's great compendium, *The Encyclopaedia of Executions* (see Bibliography). Spies were executed there during both world wars. Also as a printed source, see *The Tower of London* by Sir George Younghusband.

Newspapers and related literature

Newspapers between the eighteenth century and the twentieth are now freely available online and they present the most useful first stage in an enquiry about an offender. The tests covered range from arrest, description of the crime, trial proceedings and sometimes, accounts of family and social context. The procedure in using this resource is:

1. You need to have the name of the person and a range of dates
Or you may have the specific date of the crime.

2. Search with the assizes named
So for John Smith, who you know broke the law around 1865 and in Lincolnshire, search 'Lincoln assizes – between c.1860–1870'.

3. If you find that trial report, follow the events to the result

4. If a conviction ensues, the prison may be named
In this example, this is almost certainly (at that date) the prison inside Lincoln Castle, the Georgian prison.

A typical assize report, for a trial of average importance and complexity, will be a few paragraphs. Here is an extract from one:

> *Northern Circuit: York Winter Assizes Dec. 19*
> *Before Mr Justice Coleridge*
> *The Queen v McIntyre*
> *The prisoner is indicted for the murder of Nancy McIntyre, his wife, by kicking her. Mr Locking, a surgeon, in his examination, said that the deceased had died from kicks. He gave her brandy to restore her ... The death might have occurred from the brandy getting into the lungs ...*

From this, it may be seen that an assize report gives a fair amount of detail about the crime. Often, key questions and answers in the court questioning are also included, depending on the magnitude or complexity of the offence being dealt with.

Other periodicals also have court reports similar to the newspaper ones, and the most widespread examples are *The Gentleman's Magazine* and *The Annual Register*. These print fairly detailed accounts of trials, particularly at the assizes. For some years, in the 1850s, Charles Dickens managed a journal called *The Household Narrative*, and this also had assize reports and features on cases. A typical example is a 300-word feature which summarised the action in court and the verdict. This is the closing paragraph from a case in 1850:

> *His Lordship told them that they must find him guilty of murder if they thought he advised the giving of poison. They brought in a verdict of guilty accordingly; the judge passed sentence of death. His execution was fixed for the 17th but he received a reprieve.*

The Annual Register

This reference work is still going, but for family history purposes the earlier years of its volumes are of major interest. It began in 1758, edited by the famous thinker Edmund Burke, and it provided voluminous information on each year's events.

A typical volume – I am using the one for 1821 – has a history of Europe in great detail, extending to over fourteen small-print chapters; this is followed by the 'Chronicle' section, then a sequence of specialist reports covering a range of topics from history to travels and public documents. For present purposes, the relevant sections are 'Remarkable Trials and Law Cases' and also 'Public Documents'.

The 1821 volume has seventeen court trial reports, and these are in considerable detail. There are assize reports, so with the name and date of the ancestor, there is something here to add to any brief newspaper report. There is an index in each issue, and if the entry for 'murder' is made then we have, for example 'J. Mason, by his brother' and the information that this took place at Pateley Bridge, near Ripon in Yorkshire. *The Annual Register* has a long report on the initial inquest, and the verdict is:

> *the jury returned a verdict of wilful murder against Joseph Mason, who was committed to York Castle to take his trial. The prisoner had been previously confined for lunacy and charity would hope that this dreadful deed has been the result of some maniacal excitement.*

It is interesting to note that this took place only eight years before another insane person attempted to burn down York Minster: Jonathan Martin, whose story has been told in print many times.

It can be seen from this that *The Annual Register* gives us the inquest (found by starting research with the index) and then the link to York Castle for the trial. Mr Mason, being at York, was in the city where, at that time, the advanced care for the mentally ill was innovative and considerate, as the York Retreat was in operation. He was destined to go there rather than to prison at York, where most likely typhus would have taken him.

The Annual Register also reported on prison and prisoners; brief reports were given of such topics as escapes, scandals, appointments etc. Moreover, some volumes had accounts of prison reports, as did *The Gentleman's Magazine*. The archive is now fully searchable online at https://onlinebooks.library.upenn.edu.

THE
ANNUAL REGISTER,
OR A VIEW OF THE
HISTORY,
POLITICS,
AND
LITERATURE,
OF THE YEAR
1821.

LONDON:
PRINTED FOR BALDWIN, CRADOCK, AND JOY;
RIDGE AND RACKHAM; J. CUTHELL; LONGMAN, HURST, REES, ORME
AND BROWN; E. JEFFERY AND SON; HARDING, MAVOR, AND LEPARD;
J. BELL; SHERWOOD, NEELY, AND JONES; T. HAMILTON; G. AND W. P.
WHITTAKER; R. SAUNDERS; W. REYNOLDS; AND SIMPKIN AND MARSHALL.

1822.

Frontispiece to The Annual Register, *which contained detailed trial and crime reports for the years 1758 until well into the twentieth century. (Author)*

The Police Gazette and Illustrated Police News

This is an entry from the *Police Gazette* for November, 1916:

> *In custody at Bradford, W.R. charged with obtaining 15s by fraud, JOHN WILLIAM MARSHALL c r o no. 392-0 Ht 5' 6" c fresh h. Brown e brown tattoo mark on arm. A hawker, native of Bradford. Previous offences: shopbreaking, larceny.*

There is a great deal of information here for the researcher. We have a good profile of the man, and in fact the details show the results of the revolution in record-keeping created after the Habitual Criminals Act of 1869. He has a 'c r o' – a criminal record office number. Professionals in the criminal justice system have a hook on which to hang Mr Marshall's name.

The Police Gazette is an invaluable resource for tracing prisoner ancestors. It began in 1772 as *The Quarterly Pursuit* and was the brainchild of John Fielding, magistrate and brother to the famous novelist Henry. Later, the title changed again, first to *The Public Hue and Cry* and then simply *Hue and Cry*. It was in 1839, after the establishment of the Metropolitan Police, that it became known as *The Police Gazette*.

These volumes were digitised at the British Newspaper Archive in 2016. Some volumes are available on Ancestry. A typical example is an issue from 1829. The contents include reports of crimes by topic: murder, arson and wilful burning, house-breaking, horse and cattle stealing, larceny, frauds and aggravated misdemeanours, miscellaneous information, and property stolen. Then there is a double spread listing 'deserters from His Majesty's Service'. On the back page of the four-page folded sheet we have paragraph reports of stolen items, and finally boxed listings of charges at all the London police offices. This is an ideal place to look for the prisoner found probably initially on a prison calendar or register.

The information given of charges at police offices relates to newspaper reports of course, but the material is more prominent here. Also, the next step in the process is always given, so the researcher has a 'lead'. The detective work in family history is rarely more apparent than in working out what consequences come after a charge, and then later, after a trial. The *Gazette* reports also give a good idea of the narratives behind the facts, as in the distinctions between those going to trial and those who 'turn King's evidence'. One issue of the *Gazette* gives the reader an overall picture of police work in its context. The Gazette was a central communication device in a world which was increasingly relying on print, as today we use the internet.

CHARGES.

BOW STREET OFFICE.
NOVEMBER 7.
WILLIAM JOSEPH BANES, and CATHARINE BANES, on re-examination, with stealing one watch, six table-spoons, several dessert-spoons, and various other articles, the property of Thomas Hyde Villiers, Esq., M. P., in his dwelling-house, in Great Ryder-street, Saint James.— William Joseph Banes, committed to Newgate for trial; Catharine Banes, remanded until Saturday next.

NOVEMBER 9.
DANIEL BRYAN, with stealing one handkerchief, the property of Charles Clarkson, from his person, in Great Russell-street.—Committed to Tothill-fields Bridewell for trial.
WILLIAM HARRIS, with feloniously being at large, without any lawful cause, at Croydon, in the county of Surrey, before the expiration of a term for which he had been ordered to be transported.—Committed for trial, at the next Surrey Assizes.

NOVEMBER 10.
JAMES SEELIE, re-examined, with stealing one cheese, the property of James Lee, in Hungerford-street, Strand.— Committed to Newgate for trial.
ROBERT CLARK, re-examined, with stealing one stone mason's pick, the property of William Cubitt, in Covent-garden.—Committed to Newgate for trial.

QUEEN SQUARE OFFICE.
NOVEMBER 9.
JOHN EDWARDS, on suspicion of stealing one sieve, and a quantity of biscuits, the property of Thomas Duncan. —Committed to Newgate for trial.

MARLBOROUGH STREET OFFICE.
NOVEMBER 7.
JOHN HURDIMAN, with stealing three pieces of leather, value ninepence, the property of Alfred Rymer, of No. 10, Nassau-street, Newport-market.—Committed to Tothill-fields Bridewell for trial.

NOVEMBER 9.
FREDERICK RICHARDS, with stealing one handkerchief, of the value of two shillings, the property of a man unknown, from his person.—Committed for trial, at the next Westminster Sessions.
GEORGE KEMP, re-examined, on suspicion of stealing thirty pictures, of the value of four hundred pounds, the property of John Hewitson.—Remanded until Thursday next.
WILLIAM ALEXANDER MALCOLM, re-examined, on suspicion of receiving the same, well knowing them to have been stolen.—Remanded until Thursday next.

NOVEMBER 10.
REBECCA REYNOLDS, with stealing two printed books, of the value of two shillings, the property of Charles Stenson.—Committed to the New Prison, Clerkenwell, for trial, at the next Middlesex Sessions.

MARYLEBONE OFFICE.
NOVEMBER 7.
MARY SMITH, with stealing two half-crowns and two shillings, the monies of John Stennett, in Marylebone.— Committed to Newgate for trial.
WILLIAM PAYN, with stealing two hats, the property of William Silk (of Webber-street, Lambeth), in James-street, Covent-garden.—Committed to Newgate for trial.

NOVEMBER 7.
LOUISA HOSKINS, with stealing, in the dwelling-house of John Hale, in Marylebone, four gowns, and other articles, value seven pounds, the property of Frances Needham.— Committed to Newgate for trial.

NOVEMBER 9.
DANIEL DANIEL, on re-examination, with stealing a mahogany sideboard, value four shillings, the property of Thomas Ridge, of Cumberland-street, Saint Pancras, broker.—Committed to Newgate for trial.

WORSHIP STREET OFFICE.
NOVEMBER 7.
WILLIAM SMITH, re-examined, with stealing a silk handkerchief, the property of John Boards, in Shoreditch. —Committed to Newgate for trial.

NOVEMBER 9.
WILLIAM WESTON, re-examined, with stealing a copper, the property of James Fry, at Hackney.—Committed to Newgate for trial.

NOVEMBER 10.
ELIZABETH SMITH, re-examined, with having unlawfully and knowingly uttered and tendered in payment, to Richard Waistall and others, three counterfeit half-crowns, in Shoreditch.—Committed to the New Prison for trial, for want of sureties.

LAMBETH STREET OFFICE.
NOVEMBER 7.
EDWARD PHILLIPS, and JOHN SCROGGINS, re-examined, with stealing five silk handkerchiefs, in White-chapel, the property of George Trotter.—Committed to Newgate for trial.
JOHN SCROGGINS, THOMAS BAKER, and RICHARD BOWMAN, with stealing forty yards and upwards of silk, value five pounds, the property of Thomas Matthew and Francis Eland, in their dwelling-house, at Aldgate; and JOHN JAMES, and ELIZABETH JAMES, with receiving the said silk, well knowing it to have been stolen.—Committed to Newgate: Scroggins, Baker, John James, and Elizabeth James, for trial; and Bowman, to give evidence against them.

THAMES POLICE OFFICE.
NOVEMBER 7.
WILLIAM JONES, with stealing one silk handkerchief from the person of John Henderson, this day, in East Smithfield.—Committed for trial.

UNION HALL OFFICE.
NOVEMBER 7.
JOHN BAKER, with stealing a silver watch, yesterday in the parish of Saint George the Martyr, Southwark, the property of Henry Davis.—Committed to the County Gaol for trial.

NOVEMBER 9.
ROBERT TAITE, with stealing, on the 8th of August last, in the parish of Saint Saviour, the sum of seven pounds, twelve shillings, and sixpence, received by him on account of John Firth, his master and employer.—Committed to the County Gaol for trial.
MARY BROWN, with stealing, from the person of M John William Grece, on the night of the 6th instant, in the parish of Saint George the Martyr, Southwark, one silver watch, a bag, and twelve sovereigns, the property and monies of the said John William Grece.—Committed to the County Gaol for trial.

A typical entry from The Police Gazette *useful publication, which lists deserter lists, accounts of crimes etc. (Author)*

For instance, here is the list from the Lambeth Street Office:

EDWARD PHILLIPS and JOHN SCROGGINS re-examined, with stealing five silk handkerchiefs in Whitechapel, the property of George Trotter – committed to Newgate for trial
    JOHN SCROGGINS, THOMAS BAKER and RICHARD BOWMAN with stealing forty yards and upwards of silk, value five pounds, the property of Thomas Matthews and Francis Eland at their dwelling-place at Aldgate; and JOHN JAMES and ELIZABETH JAMES with receiving the said silk, well knowing it to have been stolen – committed to Newgate: Scroggins, Baker, John and Elizabeth James, for trial; and Bowman to give evidence against them.

The paragraph reports on the front page of the *Gazette* often give the names of suspects wanted by the law, and these give precise details also, as in this from the same issue:

MURDER

JOHN MAY who has absconded, stands charged with having, on the 5th day of July last, administered some serious drug to Joanna Marchant, then living at Torrington, to procure an abortion..and from the effects of which she died ....'

Local publications

One resource which can easily be overlooked is the local publication, usually residing in the library in every town; the material regarding prisons may be in a variety of printed locations. In the first crime history work I ever wrote, on Calderdale, I came upon a series of almanacs from Victorian times. In each issue there was an account of a crime, with plenty of names given as the narratives unfolded. It proved to be a useful resource.

Journalists and amateur historians through the years have made their contributions to prison history and their writing provides an unusual and valuable source. James Burnley, a friend of Charles Dickens who was a journalist in Bradford in the last decades of the nineteenth century, collected his essays and reports in a number of volumes, printed in London; one of his long essays was on Wakefield prison (see Bibliography) and he gives the reader an account of a lengthy tour around the inside of the prison c.1880.

Then there are the almost countless monographs, often published locally and listed in the catalogues of town libraries; many of these focus on one prison and give a thorough account of the establishment. A classic example is *The Blockhouses of Kingston-upon-Hull* by Joseph Hirst, published in 1913. This is an account of the shore-side gaols used in the Tudor period as blockhouse prisons, mainly for Catholic recusants.

Hirst explains the background to the gaols and the problems faced by the recusants, and then proceeds to bring together lists and biographies, from Tudor records, of the prisoners. This is a typical list, taken from a source in 1597 which is headed 'imprisoned in various places' and includes approximate ages:

John Cumberland, priest, 80
D. Wright, priest, D.D. 80
D. Thomas Bedell, priest, 60
D. John Almond, priest, 70
D. Robert Williamson, priest, 60
John Terry, schoolmaster, 40
Francis Parkinson, layman, 40
John Fletcher, layman.
William Tesmond
Seven others.

The volume gives information which otherwise would have had to be found in obscure records. For instance, there is the case of Roger Tocketts: due to be granted temporary liberty on a licence, for a massive fee of £200. Hill refers to the case and quotes a letter from Hull Corporation. The letter ends with:

I would require you to take bond of him in the sum of some £200 to appear presently before the Commissioners Ecclesiastical heare that further bond may be taken of him, and that he shall not depart without licence ...

As Hirst sums up, 'Roger Tocketts never got a licence. Queen Elizabeth seized all his possessions in 1599 and he remained a prisoner at Hull until his death.'

The Prison Rules
Another secondary document which is arguably the most informative way to understand the ancestor's life behind bars is the document known as *The Prison Rules*.

This is a government publication – a statutory instrument – that lists and defines the rules operating in a prison regime. For instance, a typical document covers topics on behaviour of prisoners and on their rights; medical provision; physical welfare and work; letters and visits; offences against discipline and preventive detention. Rules also cover the behaviour of officers, visiting groups and other persons having access to prisons.

The rules give a very vivid picture of prison life at a particular time. In 1964, for instance, there were twenty-one offences against discipline and four disciplinary charges. Seven paragraphs were devoted to notes on restraints. These reflect an age in which there were serious problems in prison order and control, and escapes had been common throughout the previous fifteen years.

These came in after the Prison Act of 1952, and the 1964 Rules were superseded by a new formulation in 1999.

Home Office documents

There are countless problems associated with the regime of a prison, and there always have been. The task of managing hundreds of people in round-the-clock discipline, work and care is of the greatest complexity and magnitude. In the modern prison, from the mid-nineteenth century, this became much more of a problem than it was earlier, with the bridewell/local gaol establishment. The reason for this is that there was, by Victorian times, as much emphasis on management as there was on retribution. Yes, there was still flogging and there was still the treadwheel, the latter until the last few years of the century, but inmates now had to be subject to any one of a number of management measures.

This raises the question of what back-up planning there was for the prison governor and his staff. The back-up was the provision for extraordinary cases: people and circumstances beyond the norm. In the first few decades of the nineteenth century, one such recurrent problem had been the treatment and status of political prisoners, as opposed to criminally convicted prisoners. The Chartists, for instance, who were imprisoned for their part in public disorder during the campaign for suffrage reform mostly in the 1830s, saw their incarceration as the punishment for political acts. They wanted to distinguish between their convictions and the common run of thieves and killers.

One of the most important events of this kind was the trouble caused by the Chartist prisoners, notably by William Martin. What has become known as the Sheffield Plot of 1840 involved Samuel Holberry, William Martin, Thomas Booker and others devising an attempted coup in

Sheffield in which they planned to seize the town hall and the Fortune Inn, set fire to the magistrate's court, and then, linking with other Chartists, form an insurrection also in Nottingham and Rotherham. Their plot was betrayed by James Allen and Lord Howard, the Lord Lieutenant, took immediate action. The result was that, at York Assizes on 22 March 1840, Holberry was sentenced to four years at Northallerton for seditious conspiracy: 'and at the expiration of that period to be bound himself in £50 and to find two sureties in ten shillings each, to keep the peace towards his Majesty's subjects'. He was leniently treated; under an Act of 1351 he could have had life imprisonment.

The Chartists wanted electoral reform and mainly worked for votes for working men, along with the reform of electoral districts. In the years around 1840, the 'Physical Force' arm of that movement was accelerating and the Sheffield men were out to take extreme measures. William Martin was given a sentence of one year at Northallerton and he became such a problem that the issue reached parliament. His charge was seditious language and his behaviour in court tells us a great deal about the man. *The Times* reported:

> *On sentence being passed, he struck his hand on the front of the dock, saying, 'Well that will produce a revolution, if anything will'. He begged his Lordship not to send him to Northallerton, but to let him remain in the castle at York, saying that he was very comfortable, and having been seven months confined already was quite at home.*

That was a certain way to open up the Northallerton sojourn, as the judges came down hard on Chartists and they would have had no consideration for these radicals' comfort. To Northallerton Martin went, and there he was to stir things up. In court he had already stressed his Irish connections and made reference to Irish issues: he entered into 'a long harangue' on Orangemen, the King of Hanover and Rathcormac.

Martin refused to work on the treadmill as he had not been sentenced to hard labour and so such a punishment did not fall into that category. He was put into the refractory cell for that refusal, but his case was supported by the Secretary of State, Lord Normanby, who wrote that:

> *the prisoner, who was not sentenced to hard labour, cannot legally be placed upon the wheel against his consent ... and that if he should refuse to labour upon the wheel, it would be illegal for the gaoler to place him in solitary confinement.*

But a visiting magistrate argued against this by quoting one of Peel's recent Gaol Acts which allowed for the work done on a treadmill to be defined as either hard labour or as 'employment for those who are required by law to work for their maintenance ...'

Martin, as far as we know, was compelled to work on the mill, and he claimed savage treatment at the hands of the Northallerton staff:

> One morning as soon as I had left my cell, the Governor's son ... took me by the collar and dragged me from the place where I stood and threw me with violence against the wall, and on the following day he told me I must expect different treatment from what I received in York and he added that men had been reduced to mere skeletons when their term of imprisonment expired and that it should be the case with me ...

These local problems in the treatment of prisoners who had committed 'political' crimes such as sedition, libel or even breaches of the Combination Acts or been involved in illegal trade unions, were the same everywhere; Beverley house of correction had exactly the same issues with their Chartist, Peddie, from Bradford. But leaving politics aside, the fact was that many of these agitators were involved in firearms and some had every intention of pointing their guns at police constables: some pulled the triggers.

These types of issues generated the correspondence which gathered around an individual inmate's sentence.

The Home Office, created in 1782, always had a crucial part to play in the handling of important, high profile prisoners, and it also became the port of call when it came to cries for help and advice. A letter of 1849, for instance, from the governor of Newgate, asks the Home Office for help with two prisoners who were most 'refractory and incorrigible'. They were 'creating the utmost danger to the officers' and the governor wanted something done.

The letter asking for help is simply one of hundreds of different topics which will have created a paper trail, and the same applies to the Director of Public Prosecutions. We might also include in this the prison governors, and their correspondence. All these documents offer the researcher a range of information about prisoners, as of course, the documents almost always name the inmates concerned.

At The National Archives the HO 12 series has are correspondence papers; many of the topics may be very trivial, but the subjects had to be dealt with. One letter simply has this: 'Sir, I have returned to you this day per L&N a dress case, your property, which was sent to this prison, the property of .... please acknowledge receipt of the attached.'

More commonly, the HO 21 series has entry books which deal with letters out of the prison, relating to transfers, arrivals, treatment on discharge, and also, as inspections became more and more common, to inspection visits. Governors quite rightly wanted to respond to reports on their prisons, and write on the perceived shortcomings and provision. HO 45 also has correspondence of this type.

Sometimes, the correspondence is from inmates, and these can be dramatic:

> *My dear brother ... I am sorry to state that I am sentenced to death, I am also sorry to tell you it was a parcel of lies I told you in Shepton Mallet prison ...*

Case study: Louie Calvert/police files

What has not been stressed so far is the necessity of seeing and understanding any police files relating to your ancestor. For petty crimes there will be little of course, but for the repeat offender and for serious crime, the files may well be voluminous. The following is a murder story, and so the police file has plenty of witness statements, and the files are in the archives at The National Archives and in the West Yorkshire records at Wakefield.

Lily Waterhouse was forty years old in 1923, when Louie Calvert knocked on her door. Lily's husband had died a year before, and she had lived in Amberley Road in Leeds for fourteen years. She had no idea that Calvert had come to stay with her as part of a ruse to fool her husband, Arty, into thinking that she was with her sister in Dewsbury, and that she was having a baby. Louie Calvert was indulging in one of her complex deceptions, as she was not only leading a life of deep ambiguity, but she was also a person who enjoyed lying so that she could get the thrill of escape from a mundane life.

Louie had been a housekeeper for a Mr Frobisher the year before this, and that man was found dead in the River Aire in July 1922. With hindsight it seems peculiar that the coroner did not ask more questions about the corpse. There was a wound on the back of his head and he had no boots on. At the inquest, little Louie appeared and stated that she had pawned the boots for a few shillings. All this was very strange because Frobisher lived a mile or so away from where his body was found. Had he walked barefoot to his death? Was it suicide? It is astounding that the verdict at the inquest was 'death by misadventure'.

Louie Calvert thus entered the records and she was destined to be far more prominent than that. She moved on from Frobisher's place to marry Arty Calvert in Hunslet and now there she was, away from home, pretending to be pregnant. She had two children already: one living with her and Arty, Kenneth; and a girl, Annie, who lived in Dewsbury. So here then was a strange situation: a woman of thirty-three turning up, wanting a room, and then, unknown to the landlady, the guest was trying to work out how to obtain a baby that she could pass off as her own. The obvious thing to do was to advertise, as you would for any goods. The advert in the Leeds paper did indeed work.

A teenager from Pontefract had given birth to a little girl in Leeds and her mother saw Louie's advert. It did not take long to arrange for an adoption; all Louie had to do was lie low in her lodgings and wait until the baby was with her. In this phase of her life we see Louie Calvert the odd performer, acting a role in the community. The situation was extremely bizarre: here was a married woman living under an assumed identity in another part of the same city as her husband and real home, pretending to be there in order to care for her newborn baby, who was currently in hospital. Yet strangely that would have seemed a plausible tale; at the time many young babies were ill with all kinds of maladies, from diphtheria to scarlet fever. Clearly, many would be in hospital, and the mother would visit.

Louie's love of performance, of escaping from herself and going into a role, was changing; formerly, when she worked for Frobisher, she wore Salvation Army clothes and acted the part well. But as if her life were a feature in a B movie of the time, deception led to more problems in the Waterhouse home. This sprang from the fact that Louie was a compulsive thief, and her pawning of Frobisher's boots had been just one of many visits to the pawnbroker's with items stolen. Another startling aspect of Louie Calvert is that, although she was very short and thin, in fact just five feet tall, her personality was forceful and assertive. She was capable of instilling fear in people, using sheer egoistic control and toughness. So much was this evident to Mrs Waterhouse that she was at first frightened to say anything when she began to notice that various objects had disappeared from her home.

But she gathered some determination when she found pawn tickets clearly relating to the objects missing. This was a time, of course, when many working people were in dire straits and habits such as pawning a best Sunday suit on an almost weekly basis was one desperate way of keeping a little ready cash in the house. Louie was reported to the police and was in court answering charges, but she returned to her lodgings, packed her bags and her baby, and went home to Calvert's house in Railway Place, Hunslet. As earlier writers on the amazing diminutive Calvert have speculated, how on earth she managed to be so prominent and sociable around Leeds in the time she was supposed to be having a child in Dewsbury is amazing; she was a familiar sight to many, and being distinctive in her build and her speech, she would have been seen by people passing from one area of Leeds to another, perhaps commuting.

But before Louie Calvert was to leave to go home to her husband, she had some business to attend to in Amberley Road, and it was a deadly affair. It was all brutality and lies with her, and she was clever with it.

It was just before Easter when Louie left the Waterhouse home, and Lily had been seen going into her house one Wednesday night around that time; but in those terraces neighbours saw and heard a great deal; there was very little privacy and people were sensitive to any unusual sounds. Domestic arguments would be heard by several neighbours, for instance. On this occasion, a neighbour heard noises in the lodger's room and then saw Louie as she left the house, carrying her baby. She told the neighbour that Lily was upset, but that she (Louie) was going home. She explained the odd noises by lying that she and Lily had been moving a bed.

At last Arty Calvert had his wife back, and also what he thought was his baby, little Dorothy. There was a happy time of course, and they were up late. But the next morning Arty saw that there was some luggage in the house that had not been there the night before. Unbelievably, Louie Calvert had returned to Amberley Road in the early hours and had collected a large suitcase; at this stage in her career, Louie was clumsy. She was seen by several people, despite the early time of day, and these sightings would be valuable statements later on in the tale. Even more surprising as we reread the case today, she left a note. If she had not done that, then the chances are that the dual life she had constructed might have kept her anonymous when the police started looking for the little woman who had lodged in Amberley Road.

They did indeed start looking for her, very soon after her dawn appearance at the lodgings, and this was because Lily Waterhouse had, of course, started a paper trail for the police when she summonsed her tenant. When Lily did not appear for that, the police came to check on her. What they found in her home was the woman's corpse, lying on the floor in a bedroom; there was plenty of her blood in evidence around the body, even to the extent that some blood had splashed on the wall. She had been battered on the head as there was dried blood clotted on her scalp.

The hallmark was there at the scene, though it was not perceived at the time: Lily Waterhouse was fully dressed – apart from her boots. There had been a violent struggle and the old lady had fought with some tenacity, as she was badly bruised, and it had taken several heavy blows to finish her. It is somewhat difficult to accept, bearing in mind the physical stature of Louie, that Lily Waterhouse had also been strangled. The killer, the police noticed, had cut up cloth to use to tie hands and feet; yet there must have been something else used to strangle the woman as the ligature marks on her neck were wider than those caused by a strip of cloth. It is a gruesome thought that the noises heard by the neighbours were almost certainly the movements of the dying woman's limbs as she was shaking in her death-throes. Her murderous lodger, small though she was, had been binding her tight, in an effort to stop the noises made by her feet; neighbours would certainly have heard the sounds, and would have come to ask questions. One important detail here is that the room was not carpeted. The sounds of feet thrashing on wooden boards could surely have meant that the murderer would have been disturbed as people responded to the noises heard through paper-thin walls.

What previously has been read as a widow leading a lonely and rather impoverished lifestyle turned out to be something very different as questions were asked in the ensuing investigation. In fact, some of Lily's previous lodgers had been ladies of the night; these were tough times in Leeds and there was high unemployment. A widow with a low income would no doubt have been tempted to take in guests who would pay well, and no questions would be asked. But Lily was also unusual in that she had not been the isolated figure one might suppose. She had, since her husband's death, had lots of visitors and had lived quite an interesting life, including dabbling in spiritualism. Neighbours, answering questions about her character, seemed eager to mention the shadier side of Lily's life, even to the point of one commenting that 'she was not a clean woman'. Understandably, these comments and implications about the victim led the police to look for suspects among the clientele she had mixed with in the recent past.

But then people began to recall the lodger with the baby, and there was the matter of the letter Louie had left. It was a letter about the deceit over the birth supposedly in Dewsbury. As this was addressed to Mrs Louise Calvert, there was a lead there. She was soon to be tracked down, and this woman, who had been enjoying the strange thrills of moving from one name and identity to another for some time, escaping the reality she perhaps feared, opened her door one night in April 1925 to find D.I. Pass standing there. As has been remarked previously, Louise was an unprepossessing sight, and there was a terrible irony in the fact that one of her assumed names had been Edith Thompson, the celebrated poisoner who had been hanged at Holloway in 1923; the irony is that whereas Edith Thompson was sophisticated and articulate, with a real presence, little Louise Calvert was ill-looking, underweight and coarse. Amazingly, Louise was wearing Mrs Waterhouse's boots when she answered the door. The beginning of the end for her criminal career was at hand.

The police work was extremely efficient; after Louise had covered up the questionable behaviour when she went to the Waterhouse home with a response of both nonchalance and surprise, saying 'Oh, did she do herself in then?' the police went to work on the adoption and the Dewsbury connection. She was arrested and taken away, and at that point we have to speculate about poor Kenneth and Arty Calvert. The latter had just learned that his baby was not his, and was now wondering why his wife was in the police station. Poor little Kenneth was now without his mother. At the Town Hall, Arty learned all the real facts for the first time, and while he was absorbing all that, Louise was insisting that, when charged with murder, she didn't do it.

The records relating to this case, as Louie Calvert was a prisoner in Strangeways, are varied and interesting. This is a check-list:

- Letters regarding clothing left in Leeds
- A prison notebook
- Home Office correspondence
- Material on her petition and appeal
- The police enquiries

Louie Calvert. A typical criminal record from the twentieth century. (Author)

Naturally, this is a murder case, but for any serious crime there will be material on the prison life of the ancestor. Yet equally, any prison records which reflect incidents, correspondence or inspections, will have a paper trail. With serious crimes, the investigations, the court papers and any number of testimonies and expert communications will often impinge on the main records, and so if you do have an ancestor who committed a serious crime, be prepared for anything in any area of life to emerge as you follow the repercussions of a trial or a prison event. In Calvert's case, she produced something very rare and special: a notebook with a biographical account, for future descendants to peruse.

In the most significant prisons, such as the Tower, of course there are plenty of these secondary documents in the archives.

Conclusions and summary of approaches

The survey of sources and methods has shown the notable aspects of researching prisoners' lives: the piecemeal nature of the records; the need to read laterally in a time-period, to find records outside penal documents, and also to try lesser crime/legal records. On top of this, there are all the secondary sources, those found outside the prison records.

My own first attempts to research a historical crime were made without full knowledge of just how far prison literature extends after c.1820, and more so after c.1870. In later work, I began to see how a tranche of paper trail material could be present, to build on the bare listings of the calendars.

With these thoughts in mind, it is useful here to recap. A purposeful way to do this is to summarise the experience of a prison sentence given to a felon (not a debtor) at certain periods. I am using the city of Lincoln as the anchor for these summaries.

Records: court and pipe rolls, or city records
Mediaeval –pre-assizes: He would be detained only to await trial. Conditions would be grim, as he would have been kept in the Guildhall if his offence was within the city, not the county. This was a basement-level dungeon, below the main street. There was little thought given to sustenance or care.

Records: in the records of courts, aldermen or pipe rolls
Mediaeval – post-assizes: He would now be recorded in the records of assize courts, or before this, at courts of the eyres, which met three times a year. His prison spell would be in the period between the visits of the travelling royal justices.

Records: records of assizes
Tudor/Stuart: The bridewell arrived. He would be kept in the felons' side and made to work unless he was too disabled to move. This was a house of correction. But for many wealthier people, there would be other courts of all kinds, many being political, in the age of the Reformation. For instance, the Court of Star Chamber. These had long existed before 1487, but at that date they were revised and they tried, without a jury, offences of public disorder. They were abolished in 1640.

Records: In regional record offices/archives for local gaols; for Star Chamber, records are scattered across many archives, but at The National Archives at STAC1 to STAC 10 they are listed in the catalogue. For instance, the Chancery files at the National Archives cover the years 1580–1633.
Georgian/Regency: His stay in a local gaol or in a London gaol would create more record-keeping. But still no main reforms had any impact. The first important reforms, coming in the 1820s, took a long time to have any effect.

Records: all mainstream courts from quarter sessions to the high court and Old Bailey
Victorian: Now he would be in a larger gaol, or even a convict prison. The records begin to proliferate. There would be much more information on him in secondary literature.

Records: more in the mainstream, from all levels of courts
Twentieth century: He will now be subject to any number of documents but many are restricted access. There are privacy concerns, especially after 1945; from 1907 there is even a court of criminal appeal, so more records are generated there. Juvenile courts and also different routes through the system for those considered insane are established. Also, from 1971, assizes are replaced by crown courts.

Records: All mainstream
The reader will perhaps conclude that there are two main approaches to investigating the prison experience of ancestors: the first concentrates on the prison records *per se*, relying mainly on the calendars and returns; the second looks to integrate the wider cultural and social influences from the start. Before prison sentences were regulated and fully recorded, the bare accounts, such as the manorial and pipe rolls, reflected merely the few people involved around an accusation and a verdict. The main record was often final in terms of the paper trail of that person.

The perfect concomitant of family history paper-based research or internet research is to visit the actual site of the ancestor's detention. In Britain, our few remaining Victorian or Georgian prisons are rarely preserved in such a state that they may be visited, but there are examples such as Oxford prison, which is now a hotel, or the old Lincoln Georgian prison, now an important part of the city's heritage trail, along with the mediaeval gaol in the city at the Stonebow.

Some old prisons, long out of use, are now used for educational tours, and there is no better way to appreciate an ancestor's prison experience than to see the cells, landings and wings of past gaols. An example of this is Stafford (see prison information at www.justice.gov.uk).

But some of these prisons have gone, such as Northallerton, the subject of one of my case studies, or the house of correction at Beverley. However, there are several books in print which relate the histories of many local prisons and of the main convict prisons, or give an insider's view, having been prisoners inside. Readers are directed to these, and here is a sample of the most thorough:

Burford, E.J., *In the Clink* (New English Library, 1977)
Byrne, Gerald, *Borstal Boy: the uncensored story of Neville Heath* (Headline, 1947)
Chalkin, C.W., (Editor) *New Maidstone Gaol Order Book 1805-1823* (Kent Archaeological Society, 1984)
Disney, Francis, *Heritage of a Prison: HMP Shepton Mallet, 1610-1985* (Self, 2008)
Douglas, Robert, *At Her Majesty's Pleasure* (Hodder, 2008)
Goodall, Peter J.R., *For Whom the Bell Tolls* (Gomer, 2001)
Halliday, Stephen, *Newgate: London's Prototype of Hell* (History Press, 2007)
Harris, Vernon, *Dartmoor Prison, Past and Present* (Leopold Classic Library, 2015)
James, Erwin, *A Life Inside: a prisoner's notebook* (Atlantic Books, 2003)
Jeffrey, Robert, *The Barlinnie Story* (Black and White, 2009)
Jowett, Caroline, *The History of Newgate Prison* (Pen and Sword, 2017)
Joy, Ron, *Dartmoor Prison: At Her Majesty's Pleasure* (Halsgrove, 2002)
Lonsdale, Dame Kathleen, and Page, Roger, *Some Account of Life in Holloway Prison for Women* (Prison Medical Reform Council, 1943)
Lytton, Constance, *Prisons and Prisoners* (1914) (Virago, 1988)
Maxwell, Richard, *Borstal and Better* (Hollis and Carter, 1956)
Owens, Lewis, *The Pentonville Experiment: Prison, Addiction, Hope* (Self, 2018)

Stokes, Anthony, *Pit of Shame: the real ballad of Reading Gaol* (Waterside, 2007)

Wade, Stephen, *House of Care* (Bar None Books, 2008)

Wade, Stephen, *Stones of Law and a Square of Hedon Sky* (Bar None Books, 2010)

Chapter 11

CRIMINAL OFFENCES

As a starting-point for a reference section, it is helpful for historians and researchers to have a grasp of what the commonest criminal offences were throughout crime history. Some are generally known, but other need clear definition. Some offences have gone, of course, and others have been modified or redefined. A good basic law dictionary is useful to researchers, but the following notes are a first step in understanding the crimes found in documents and records.

The foregoing chapters have demonstrated that prisoner records in Britain face the researcher and historian with a threefold task:

1. Ascertain what, when and where? This is regarding the offence.
2. Understand the prison and the sentence
3. List and collect all documentation

First, before anything else, there is the question of what exactly the offence was.

In the monumental work by Blackstone, *Commentaries on the Laws of England* (1765), he deals with law under headings of *rights of persons, the rights of things, private wrongs and public wrongs*. The offences we are all familiar with from crime fiction and television drama are only loosely understood by laypeople. The *Commentaries* provided a guide, for law students and general readers alike, to specific actions regarded as transgressions within the common law.

First a basic distinction between misdemeanours and felonies needs to be given.

- *Misdemeanour:* An offence which was punishable by fine and imprisonment. Statutes define the various misdemeanours.

- *Felony:* an offence which was punished by the forfeiture of land and goods.

This is a huge difference of course. For instance, treason would be a felony, with the offender losing everything. Felony was removed and abolished in 1967.

Assault/battery
Blackstone has 'an attempt to offer to beat another, but without touching him'. This opens up the ability to want redress by the one assaulted. Whereas battery is unlawful beating of another person. Most dictionies of law comment that the use of the word 'assault' implies a battery.

Burglary
Formerly, housebreaking by night, between the hours of 9pm and 6pm. The 1968 Theft Act changed this by widening the definition to the notion of a person breaking and entering as a trespasser with an intent to commit offences.

Concealing a birth
This was, before 1861, a felony, as it related to infanticide; then the Offences against the Person Act made it a misdemeanour.

Desertion
This offence is removing oneself from the status of being a serving person in the armed forces, without having a licence to be freed from that contract. In 1957 an Act made it clear that leaving with an intention of making the separation permanent defined it.

Forgery
This is the creation of a false document to pass it off as being genuine. The Forgery Act of 1913 consolidated other offences related to the basic definition.

Fraud
The standard wording is: 'Something said, done or omitted by a person with the design of perpetrating what he or she must know was a positive fraud.'

Infanticide
The killing of a child by its mother was a branch of murder until the Infanticide Act of 1938. This provided for the 'while of unsound mind' proviso, and so placed infanticide on a level with manslaughter.

Larceny
'The unlawful taking and carrying away of things personal, with intent to deprive the right owner of the same.' The Theft Act of 1968 removed larceny, repealing the Larceny Acts of earlier years.

Manslaughter
The unlawful killing of another without malice express or implied. The two main varieties are *voluntary* 'upon a sudden heat', or *involuntary* – in the process of an unlawful act.

Murder
This word is so often used in popular narratives now that researchers and novelists have to be very careful when using or explaining it. Everything depends on *intention*. Hence the standard definition of 'malice aforethought'. So we have 'unlawful homicide committed with malice aforethought'.

Pornography/obscenity
By the Obscene Publications Acts of 1959 and 1964 something is said to be obscene if its use will 'deprave or corrupt' persons likely to use, read or watch the said item.

Procuring a miscarriage
This obviously relates to the subject of illegal abortions, and criminal history is littered with such cases, many of them being notorious in their time. Because, in an alleged illegal abortion case, the testimony of a dying woman in childbirth, or soon after the birth, was given without an objective witness, the accused could say anything in court. A dying declaration is a statement which may, of course, point the finger at someone present. The case of Aleck Bourne illustrates this (see *Rex v. Bourne* 1938).

Prostitution
This topic covers prostitutes, but also pimping and keeping a brothel. The word prostitution is not so easy to explain or define, though. *The Oxford English Dictionary* helps, defining a prostitute as: 'A woman who is devoted or who offers her body to indiscriminate sexual intercourse, especially for hire. A common harlot.' As so often applies, this means different things at different times, but the constant in all usages is a moral condemnation, above any legal one.

Robbery
On the surface, this is easy to define: 'A person is guilty of robbery if he steals, and immediately before or at the time of doing so, he uses force on any other person or seeks to put another person in fear.' In the records, a great importance attaches to the exact nature of a robbery. The idea of 'highway robbery' at one time was a capital offence, and so the location of the robbery was crucially important in a criminal trial. The place of the offence, either within property or out on the public highway, made an immense difference in court.

Suicide
Until 1961, suicide was a crime, and indeed a felony. After that legislation, only a suicide pact was still a crime. The ethical implications of the act go deep and wide. In the seventeenth century, a writer called Dalton explained neatly why the crime was so complex: he wrote that it was an offence 'against God, against the King and against Nature.' It may be seen from those words that in a court of law, the implications of a specific suicidal death were far-reaching and profound in their effects.

Some suicides, of course, attain far more in a criminal way than one simple death, as in a report in *The Independent* from Paris in 1986: 'A young man survived a suicide attempt yesterday, but in the process killed two, injured thirteen, and partly demolished a five-storey apartment building when he turned on gas jets in his kitchen but then decided to have a last cigarette'.

Theft
The Theft Act of 1968 states that 'a person is guilty of theft if he dishonestly appropriates property belonging to another with the intention of permanently depriving the other of it'. The point which has to be attached to this is that it is immaterial whether or not the theft is for the benefit of the thief.

Witchcraft
A general and loose definition might be that this is an alleged interaction with evil spirits. Under Acts established in 1541 and 1603, the law was enforced and as late as 1716 a woman was hanged, along with her nine-year-old daughter, for the offence. In 1735 an Act made it an offence to pursue a person and seek to accuse them of witchcraft, with a year's prison as deterrent. The Witchcraft Act of 1736 removed the offence from the statutes.

Glossary of terms in the text

This is a basic list of legal terms which tend to occur in the research process involved in finding a family 'black sheep'. Most have been in the text. These terms are more likely to be encountered on documents; the following glossary is for wider, more general terminology.

Assize courts: The various assizes on the circuits in England and Wales at which judges would hear cases twice a year – these were felonies, more serious, indictable crimes.

Calendar of prisoners: This is a document showing all essential information on convicted people: name, age, magistrate, date of custody, offence, details of the trial and sentence.

Court hand: This was a particular style of handwriting at first used by the legal professionals and put to use in the formal records of the courts of Common Pleas and King's/Queen's Bench.

Criminal register: This document gives details of convicts: repeating calendar information.

Deposition: This was an examination of the defendant and the witnesses.

Felony/misdemeanour: offences were formerly defined in the common law as felonies or misdemeanours. A felony meant the loss of land and goods until the Forfeiture Act of 1870. A misdemeanour was any offence that did not constitute a felony.

Grand jury: This was conceived at the Assize of Clarendon in 1166; the idea was that this body of an uneven number of men would make a presentment for an indictment relating to a criminal offence. If a drafted bill (indictment) was found to be a 'true bill' then the defendant would have to face a trial by the jury of twelve. If there was a not guilty decision then the bill was 'ignoramus' – there being no case to answer. The grand jury was abolished in 1948.

House of correction: The name for a local prison or 'bridewell' – both terms used interchangeably in early writings.

Indictable/summary: An offence triable since 1971 at Crown Court and formerly at assize; in contrast, a summary offence need not be heard before a jury.

Indictment: A formal statement of the charge against the accused person.

King's Bench: The highest criminal court.

Latin in assizes: Before 1733 assize records were in Latin. Later, there were still Latin abbreviations:

- *Ca null – catalla nulla* – no goods to forfeit
- *Cog ind – cognovits indictamentum* – confessed to indictment

- *Cul – culpabilis* – guilty
- *Ign – ignoramus* – no case to answer
- *Non cul nec re – non culpabilis nec retraxit* – not guilty and did not flee
- *Po se – point se super patriam* – puts himself on the country (chooses a jury trial)
- *Sus – suspendatur* – let him be hanged
- *Nisi prius* – a trial by jury with a single judge, at assizes
- *Order books* – formal records of court proceedings

Palatinate courts: The counties of Cheshire, Durham and Lancashire were known as Palatinates. Changes were made in 1830 in Cheshire; the Durham court continued until 1876 (then being amalgamated into the North Eastern Assize circuit). Lancashire also had a Palatinate court until 1876. These court records are in the Public Record Office.

Parish constable: The official responsible for law and order, before the first professional police who gradually appeared after the Police Act of 1829 which created the Metropolitan Police.

Petitions: In quarter sessions, petitions refer to bills of costs for prosecutions.

Piepowder Court: (From the French court of *piedpoudre*) Before its abolition in 1971, this court dealt with offences occurring at feasts, fairs and markets.

Plaintiff: The person prosecuting in court

Quarter sessions: The trials heard four times a year, run by justices of the peace.

Recognisance: A document binding a witness to appear at court.

Respite: A discharge – in times past, it was the reprieve given to a condemned felon by the Home Secretary.

Superior court: One of the higher level courts dealing with trials of very serious crime; these are both civil and criminal of course.

Glossary of legal terms in documents

Searching prison records also means searching court records. We naturally wish to know the trajectory of a criminal life if that life is one of our forebears. For this reason, the following is a fuller explanation of the principal legal terms which will be encountered in researching prisoners.

The history of crime and law in Britain reflects all the major elements of social and political change; what better way to understand the repercussions of important and radical forces acting on a nation or on a community than a look at the cases before the courts? There is the legal language to overcome, of course, and the layperson tends to think that law reports are written with a basis of thinking summed up in the words: why use a sentence when three chapters will do? But leaving legal vocabulary aside, the point is that the records of everyday law, civil and criminal, make for exciting, humorous and sometimes totally bizarre reading.

Pottering around my local antiques centre recently, I came across a box of old wills. Some of those documents were from three centuries ago, and were probably all about chattels and land, who inherited them and who gave them. I say probably because not only were the documents composed of very long sentences, they also had words which seemed to have been formed from a wayward mix of dead Latin and something else that the lawyers made up from a game of fridge magnet Scrabble.

I imagined the relatives sitting around the lawyer as he read out a will. Half an hour would pass, and then there would be a long silence followed by, 'Could you read that again please ... in English?'

It has always been difficult to avoid being involved in the law in some way. Even Shakespeare had to appear in court, at the Court of Requests, to testify that someone owed someone else some money. That was fortunate for the scholars in one way, but possibly not, because in the time he had to stand in court, after waiting to take his place, he could have written part four of *Henry IV* or a sequel to *Hamlet*.

The vocabulary of the law has always been intractable and baffling. As far back as Anglo-Saxon times, the early laws produced by kings in Kent and Mercia were teeming with bizarre terms such as *frankpledge*, *tithingman* and *ingfanthief*. We can imagine King Offa plotting to devise the most surreal and hard-to-pronounce Germanic words, just to confuse the rabble he had to deal with.

Lawmakers started to dream up bizarre rules such as compensation for offences: if an offence was committed on a holy day, for instance, the fine was twice as high. If a man's ear was cut off in a fight, the fine was twelve shillings; if a front tooth was knocked out, then the attacker had to pay just six shillings.

All this helps us to understand why Shakespeare produced the immortal line in *Julius Caesar*: 'Let's kill all the lawyers'. They were in as much danger as the poets when the mob was in a foul mood.

Social history has its own difficulties when we wish to read and understand events and stories from the past in which the process of law has been involved. A dictionary of law is not enough to explain to the layman hat exactly happened or what was meant by the legal language employed.

In the business of researching crime stories from the centuries of British history in which criminal justice systems came and went, and in which definitions of what was criminal shifted constantly, I came to see that readers of narrative history needed some help to find their way through the labyrinths of legal vocabulary.

A famous judge once said that, as he made his way to court that morning, he saw twenty-five crimes committed. These included everything from dangerous driving to infringement of by-laws. Of course, he could do nothing about it unless he had been in the mood to make dozens of citizens' arrests.

But in years gone by, a man could find himself battered and bewildered as much by the explanation of the crime he had committed as by the arrest and detention. Governments have a way of legislating to achieve their ends, come what may. In the worst years of the Luddite machine-smashing, in around 1812–1814, the Home Secretary needed an offence that would make it easy to stick a capital charge on the troublemakers. They had done lots of nasty things, but an offence was needed that would make sure they would swing on the gallows at York. In haste, the offence of 'taking an illegal oath' was created. They had got their men.

Hopefully, my guide and dictionary will provide explanation, along with some entertaining tales from the past. My stories perhaps confirm the wise words of Cicero: 'it is ignorance of the law rather than knowledge of it that leads to litigation'.

My aim here is to provide explanations along with the stories, but the narrative interest comes first. In my career as a true crime writer I have had to learn to understand legal process, the whole knotty business in criminal justice in which records are either in jargon or in Latin, so I have some idea what it is like to plough through tortuous sentences and levels of pomposity beyond belief. The main element of entertainment I offer here are the tales of hapless individuals through the centuries, wanting to sue someone, avoid a fine or inherit grandad's stash. My stories are sometimes of criminals but also of innocent victims, the common people caught up in social change and in the jaws of rapacious businessmen.

Yes, let me come clean here. I have no degree in law: I'm writing simply as a writer and historian who has had to struggle through masses of legal documents from past years, and so learn by mistakes and false paths. A typical example is my research for a famous murder case in Lincolnshire, in which the killer was tried at a court in Lincoln – the assizes. But one local report on the cases referred to the court being *nisi picus*. As everyone knows from television crime dramas, law is packed with Latin vocabulary, and here was an example for me. I reached for my copy of *Lawyers' Latin* by John Gray, and found no such words. Then, by a process of good luck and persistence, I discovered that the journalist had got it wrong; he meant *nisi prius*. This means 'unless before' and means that a case will be tried at the court in London unless the assize date falls before that date. It is a writ to the sheriff to gather jurors for such a trial. Now, to a layman, that was quite a challenge, and such matters face us every day, even as general readers, as the Law Reports in *The Times* illustrate every day.

With all this in mind, my little guide should be at your elbow or within reach of your seat at the desk when tackling crime and law from past times.

A

Act of God: Legally, an Act of God is applied to something that could not have been foreseen or guarded against. This story is a crazy example of that, and it saved a man from the gallows.

It reads like such a simple, uncomplicated statement of a killing: 'York Assizes: Abraham Bairstan, aged 60, was put to the bar, charged with the wilful murder of Sarah Bairstan his wife, in the parish of Bradford'. In the busy, overworked courts of the Regency, dealing with new and often puzzling crimes form the labouring classes in the fast-growing towns, it was maybe just another 'domestic' that went too far. But this is far from the truth, and the Bairstan case gives us an insight into the plight of those unfortunate people at the time who were victims of ignorance as well as of illness. In this instance it was an awful, anguished mental illness that played a major part in this murder.

When the turnkey brought Bairstan into the court he commented that he had not heard the prisoner say a word since he was brought to York and locked up. This was nothing new to the man's family. Mr Baron Hullock, presiding, was shocked but also full of natural. He pressed the gaoler to explain. He asked if the man in the dock understood the spoken word, and the answer was no. He also ascertained that Bairstan appeared to have no response to any sound whatsoever, nor any movement.

It makes painful reading in the court report to note that the prisoner was a 'dull and heavy looking man who ... cast a vacant glance around the court'. The reporter in 1824 noted that the man 'appeared totally insensible of the nature of the proceedings'.

Poor Hullock had a real challenge to try to communicate with the man, trying his best to make the prisoner make any sound at all, asking several questions but receiving no answer. When he asked 'Do you hear what I say to you?' Bairstan simply stared at the officer next to him.

It was obviously going to be one of those trials at which many people were thinking that this silence was the best ruse if a man wanted to avoid the rope. The judge had to instruct the jury about potential fraud and the possibility that this was a tough and amoral killer with a canny wit and impressive acting skills. In legal jargon, the point was, was the man standing there fraudulently, wilfully and obstinately, or 'by the act and providence of God?' It was going to be a hard task, one might think, but not so: enter his sons and a close friend. They told a very sad story, and an astounding one, given that Bairstan managed to marry and raise a family.

His friend stated that he had known the prisoner for over fifty years, and that he was sure that ten years had passed since Bairstan had fallen silent. He explained that his two sons had been looking after the old man in that time. His key statement was that 'while he was sane, his wife and he had lived together very comfortably'. The man, Jeremiah Hailey, added that his friend had been capable of merely saying yes or no, and that the last time he had heard the man speak was when he had asked him if he knew his friend Jeremiah. 'He said aye, but I think he did not know me.'

Bairstan's two sons confirmed that their father had been silent in that ten-year period, only excepting one or two words. Henry said that since being locked up, his father had been pressed to speak and had answered something sounding like. 'Be quiet ... be quiet'. The other son, Joseph, confirmed that his father had been 'out of his mind' for ten years.

There had been enough in him to marry and earn a living, but we must see with hindsight and more relevant knowledge, that Abraham Bairstan had been struck by a paralysis, perhaps combined with a depressive mental illness. In 1824, the most meaningful explanation was to put it down to God's will, so the jury found that the prisoner stood mute 'by the visitation of God'.

Or, if one is pressed to say that it had all been a wonderfully impressive family performance, then would not this be the sure way to keep the old man from the noose? On the other hand, he was destined to be shut away for ever in awful conditions, being criminally insane. The truth will perhaps never now be known.

Amercement: Usually, this was a punishment of a fine of some kind. In mediaeval times it was imposed by a court of record. The offender in question was defined as being 'at the King's mercy.'

Approver: In early mediaeval years, this was a man who had supplied information and informed of a crime. He would have to confront trial by battle.

Asylums: In terms of its usefulness to researchers in family history, the importance lies in the 1815 Act which impacted on quarter sessions. Lists of pauper lunatics were given to the bench at these sessions. Then later, after 1832, private asylums figured in these lists and in the inspection work undertaken by the magistrates.

Attainder: When parliament applied attainder, it meant that a person condemned to suffer after a capital conviction would lose all rights and privileges. This was abolished by the Forfeiture Act of 1870.

B
Bad character: The Vagrancy Act of 1824 defined a vagrant as being one of these categories of person: a) idle and disorderly, b) rogue and vagabond, c) an incorrigible rogue. In common parlance, officers of the law were in the habit of referring to some of these types as 'bad characters' and simple though that Act appears to be, a case in Grimsby illustrates the problem with it.

In English criminal law, a person standing charged with an offence has to be tried on the grounds of that specific offence, and nothing else beyond that. Courts in the past have often run into trouble and made mistakes because of contravening that rule. In the case of a known criminal in Grimsby a mistake was made.

In October 1955, Mr Fitzwalter Buller found himself acting for a group of people whose property had been under threat from a 'vagrant' named Fuller. It was going to be a simple matter to show that the man had been up to no good on some premises, as the recorder at the quarter sessions in Grimsby had been given a long list of the man's previous convictions. That was a step that the aggrieved parties may have regretted because the case went to the court of appeal.

It was a case of a record of a known 'bad character' being given in court to prejudice a decision. Fuller had been asked why he had not accepted work, as he had not appeared in court at an earlier time. Then, on the night in question, he had been found in a place where he was almost certainly going to commit an offence.

The drifter was a man who had caused a series of confrontations with the local police and he was often under observation; it was known that he was the type who could easily shift from minor offences to other, more serious ones, and when he was caught and charged on this particular occasion, that thinking lay behind the police actions, but it was in the court that things went wrong for everyone concerned, and all because of a too-enthusiastic court officer.

Fuller had been given a three-month prison sentence for that offence, under the old Vagrancy Act of 1824, so there was a feeling of certainty that he was out to do a burglary or even worse. But, as the appeal court noted, to haul him up in court and then place the list of convictions in from of the judge was malpractice. The judge at appeal said, 'The merest glance at the report by anyone accustomed to that class of document, as every recorder would be, would show him that he was dealing with what might be called "an old hand".' The mere sight of the document, it was said, would show that the appellant was a man with a long list of previous convictions.

The outcome was that if there was an appeal against a conviction, then no details of previous convictions should be made visible. The man had gone to prison on what in legal terms is called an 'unsafe' judgement. Clearly, this all became a matter of prejudice, and that was not difficult to show before the High Court Judge, Mr Justice Ormerod.

Here was a case of a 'bad character' who nevertheless found himself languishing in gaol because he had received a 'punishment' for things allegedly done well before the latest appearance in court. Maybe his defence in court – that he had been on the property when he was arrested looking for work – did not really convince the magistrate, but he was badly handled, and that was the bottom line.

The fateful list, given to the Recorder, could not have been put in front of a jury, and so a basic principle of law had been breached. The basis of the debate was in the operation of the so-called 'Sus laws' and these were common causes of discontent at the time. The famous detective Jack Slipper, on the streets at the same time as the Grimsby event, has this to say about these laws, which enabled officers to stop anyone 'on suspicion':

> *As I became more experienced I had a number of good arrests, thanks to the Section Four of the 1824 Vagrancy Act which allows a police officer to arrest someone he suspects of being about to commit an arrestable offence. That doesn't mean you can pick up someone just because he might be a criminal ...*

In other words, the Grimsby affair happened largely because the officers concerned knew the man in question. He was not 'just someone'.

Barratry: This is nothing to do with the construction of new estates and small detached houses. This offence was concerned with troublemakers. Common barratry was the offence of frequently inciting and stirring up suits and quarrels between Her Majesty's subjects. This was abolished by the Criminal Law Act of 1967. Many barrators in criminal history had interesting experiences, frequently with reference to prison life. The most frequent occurrences tend to refer to barratry on board ship: 'any wilful or fraudulent act committed by the master of a ship … causing damage to the ship or cargo …'

The famous Judge Jeffreys tried two brothers called Williamson for barratry and he had them both put in the pillory. Jeffreys' opinion of the offence was 'an offence committed by scurrilous attorneys in trumping up cases and encouraging hopeless litigation'.

C

Clipping (and uttering): These terms relate to forgery. Coins were clipped, by the snipping of the metal edges of coins, melting this down and then making more illegal coinage from the metal. Uttering was, according to the *Mozley Dictionary of Law*, 'any person knowingly uttering false coin is guilty of misdemeanour'. The Forgery Act of 1913 consolidated many offences entailing false documentation and coinage.

Compter: This was an old name used for city debtors' prisons. It comes from the old Middle English spelling of 'counter'. From this we can say 'a place where one is brought to account'. The one most frequently referred to is the Poultry Compter. For instance, the *London Gazette*, which listed insolvent debtors, has this for 2 May 1769: 'Fugitives surrendered to the Keeper of the Poultry Compter in the City of London: First notice –Levy Wolfe, formerly of Plymouth, a hawker.'

The Poultry Compter was built in the fourteenth century, and was rebuilt in 1645, then lost in the Great Fire in 1666. It was finally demolished in 1817.

Conjugal rights: This was repealed by the Matrimonial Causes Act of 1973. But for so long this was the kind of case that dragged on and created hell. It was a suit by a husband to compel a wife to live with him, or by a wife to compel a husband to take her back.

Most cases in the massive legal records relating to this are of course dull and predictable, but there are always cases to raise a smile, such as the case of Conolly v Conolly. These two Americans married in 1831, and Mr Conolly was a clergyman in the Episcopal Church of America. That seems quite straightforward, but then they both succumbed to the allure of the Catholic Church in that age of dogma and swerving faith. They not only decided to live apart, so he could follow the path of celibacy, they went to the Pope himself to have a separation granted, and Gregory XVI obliged. They then went to total extremes. Not only did the husband become a priest, but the wife became a nun, and so keen was she on her new life that she founded a religious order in Derby.

Mr Conolly, clearly a man who vacillated and doubted, following his passions and the cooling off, wished to return to the Protestant fold. The old life had to include his wife, and she was fond of her new habit, so a suit was instigated for the reverend's conjugal rights. The judge was evidently defeated by this complexity and demolished the business on the grounds that the separation at Rome had not been 'sufficiently set forth'.

Another odd tale concerns the Earl of Stair, Mr Dalrymple. He eloped with a young woman called Miss Gordon, but things turned sour for him and the marriage became a burden; he rejected her but she sued for conjugal rights. Stair was living with his new sweetheart and so his solution to the problem was to engage a lothario to court Miss Gordon, and arrange for an embarrassing situation to be come across. If that succeeded, the earl was to pay the man a large amount of cash.

What happened then was that Mrs Dalrymple sued for a divorce and had one granted, before any embarrassing situation could be arranged. The lover sent by the earl then turned cool and rebuffed her, with the result that she lost her wits and was placed in an asylum. Twenty-seven years later she regained her sanity, but her commission was superseded – the action was finally cancelled. What happened to the lothario is a mystery.

D

Doli capax: This means 'capable of crime' and indicates that in a case, a child between the ages of eight and fourteen has sufficient understanding to discern between good and evil, and so know that his or her action in a circumstance would be criminal. In years gone by, many liked to explain the 'spare the rod, spoil the child' remedy.

In January 1889, a minor episode of shoplifting in Doncaster reached the national newspapers and caused a lengthy debate. That may have been unusual for a Doncaster story, but the subject was certainly nothing new. The general public had been well informed about 'rings' of child thieves, most famously by Charles Dickens in *Oliver Twist* back in 1838, and after that year there had been a constant fear of child criminals. The main statutory measures against the problem had been the establishment of the reformatories in the 1850s. That had been one way of dealing with juvenile crime – take the little villains away from home and work them into submission!

These tough measures had not really addressed the heart of the problem. If we accept that in the history of crime drink and poverty have always been causal factors, then that was central to the Victorians, and they had those problems in the absolute extreme. The massive demographic shift of labour into the new towns after the Enclosure Acts (accelerated after 1801) and the proliferation of the factories and mills had created a general need of child labour, and education had been slow to develop as a remedial measure, something to make childhood happy and hopefully imaginative. But it has to be said that the universal influence of beer shops and the habit of drinking gin at all times was a formative tendency in making poverty a massive social issue.

The result was that the late Victorian years had new debates about children and the law. One of the commonest features of this was the context of what we now try to deal with in issuing the ASBO: children left out to roam, create trouble and fend for themselves.

This was the case in Doncaster at this time, and the story that reached the dignified pages of *The Times* was one featuring two children: a brother and sister called Margaret and Daniel Fell. They went on a stealing spree in Doncaster one day and stole £2 from a confectioner in Hall Gate called Miss Brooks. That was quite a lot of money, but matters were more serious when it was found that they had raided several other shops, averaging a few pounds in cash from each one.

The boy was ten and the girl seven; they had been taught to steal by a mysterious child called Harker, and of her there is nothing else known but her name. Margaret and Daniel took their booty and met another child, then all three decided to have a day out in Lincoln. There, they appear to have spent their takings, and not stolen anything; they went for a number of rides on the trams, and it was while on one of these that a driver became suspicious of them and called the police.

At the Doncaster Police Court, the children faced their punishment. The Chief Constable, Isaac Gregory, recounted the events of the day of the spree, and he said that their parents 'Had a good deal of trouble with these children'. He told a familiar story: that the children were never supervised and the parents never had an idea where they were; he said they were 'allowed to go prowling about at night'. It is surely unusual that the Chief Constable was there to speak. It is hardly a job for the senior police officer. Perhaps that tells us that this case was merely one of many similar ones and that juvenile crime was reaching mammoth proportions.

That appears to be the case when we consider the response to this crime. But what caused the heated response was the punishment. In Doncaster, the magistrate ordered Daniel Fell to receive 'six strokes from the birch rod', whereas Margaret received no punishment and was too young to be sent to a reformatory. The only additional action taken was that the parents (who bothered to turn up) were admonished and told to take better care of their children in future. A correspondent to *The Times* picked up the story and wrote:

> *The reason why the real thief was dismissed scot-free and her less guilty brother whipped was of course, not the one given by the magistrates … Had the girl been the child of one of the magistrates, there probably was not one of them who, when he got home, would not have given her a child's whipping.*

The author of the letter was the Earl of Meath, and he was really making a point about the reformatories and the age at which young offenders could be sent to one of those institutions. From 1854 the ruling had been that only girls under the age of sixteen could be sent to a reformatory. For children such as Daniel and Margaret, the punishment was whipping and a caution. In earlier times, public humiliation had been the punishment, with the use of stocks and pillory, but in these supposedly more enlightened times, a beating was considered to be a civilised measure. As early as 1816 there had been a Parliamentary Committee to investigate juvenile crime, but little was done; children could still be sent to prisons along with adults, and this continued until the year following this hearing in Doncaster. Just thirteen years after these Doncaster children were in court – in 1902 – the first borstal was established.

But the issue of fair punishment was still there at the time. The Earl of Meath was answered by 'a Board Master' anonymously. He argued that, 'I must join issue with him in his suggested remedy – viz., the substitution of the birch for the cane'. The schoolmaster was worried about the repercussions, saying of the birch, 'That instrument has hitherto been looked upon only as an adjunct to police courts, and its introduction into schools would, I fear, stir up popular clamour.'

J

Judges and juries: Some of the law's most curious tales have come from the records of the assize courts. In the Georgian and Victorian years, the judges had such extreme power, and they were often so notably eccentric and whimsical, that their cases generated stories which are bizarre and sometimes puzzling.

Take for instance the events of December 1857, when Mr Justice Crompton presided. Before him was a poaching case but there was a shortage of jurors. The jury foreman, Sir C.H.J. Anderson of Lea, said he was the presenter in a poaching case committed by four men on his own estate. He naturally applied to be excused duty and had arranged for another man to step in. Justice Crompton said, 'I cannot see how I can substitute one grand juryman for another after the charge has been delivered … I have never known such a thing before'. His Honour was aware that having the knight and plaintiff on his jury could be seen to be a problem, saying he wanted to avoid any impression from the lower classes that would reflect badly on the administration of justice. What was he to do? The only solution was to drop the whole affair and discharge the alleged poachers.

Then there was the strange behaviour of Mr Justice Maule, a notable character on the bench, who in 1852 complained that there was no fresh air in his court and ordered all the windows to be opened. But there was no response, so he had a fit of temper and threatened to have the windows broken if his wishes were not immediately obeyed. He passed a stout stick to a member of the jury to be used to smash the windows if he was not obeyed.

The man who could open all the windows was incredibly slow, so Mr Justice Maule wasted no time in ordering all the windows to be smashed. *The Times* reported on what happened:

> *The smashing of the glass, as it came tumbling on the heads of the people below, and peals of laughter which were in consequence elicited from the bar and the whole court, produced a scene which will be remembered by those who witnessed the occurrence. His Lordship, evidently wincing under the ridicule which his eccentric behaviour had excited, intimated, in not the most calm and dignified manner, and at the same time looking down upon the bar, that those gentlemen who wished to indulge in such indecorous behaviour had better go and indulge themselves out of the court …*

At length, the court resumed its normal business and there was no problem with the hot air.

In 1821 there had been a riot at Stamford and a certain Mr Williams was indicted for breaking windows at the home of a Mr Hunt. Although the defence lawyer argued that there had been no riot, the judge disagreed, saying that no man on his oath could say that the events had not been a riot. The jury withdrew and after two hours, eleven of the jury could agree but one man held out. Might the eleven men be discharged? The judge said that was impossible.

The jury then spent another five hours and there was no change. The resolute juryman told the court that he could not 'reconcile it to his conscience' that Mr Williams had riotously demolished the said windows. The judge would not let him withdraw. The man said, 'I would sooner eat mortar from the ceiling than give in'. With that state of affairs, the jury would have had to go with the judge to Nottingham, so they thought long and hard and finally handed in a note to the judge at the lodgings by the castle saying that they agreed for the defendant. No mortar had to be eaten that night.

M

Malfeasance: 'The commission of any act which is in itself unlawful'(Mozley and Whiteley's *Law Dictionary*) – to be understood in contrast to *nonfeasance,* which is failing to do an act a person lawfully has to do. (*neglect* in modern terms). Then we have *misfeasance,* which is the wrongful doing of an action that should be lawfully done. This is antiquated language and naturally the words with occur in old documents relating to trials and records. In the mid Victorian years, in the Court of Chancery, the case of Connor v Connor was tried. Mr Connor left some property worth £8,000. His next of kin was given the power to act on that by a church court. But a woman came forward, claiming to be the dead man's widow 'by virtue of a Scotch marriage'. She brought a suit to force the production of a marriage certificate which was in the husband's papers, to prove her status.

The Vice-Chancellor intervened to put an injunction on the administrator, to prevent any actions being taken with the property of the dead man. Messrs Parker and Prior, for the application to discharge the order, said that no interference must take place with the property 'in the absence of any malfeasance'.

Quite dull, perhaps, but this was not the case of the poachers before the judge in 1854. A writer to *The Times* pointed out that these poachers had trespassed and tried to steal. They had claimed that they were on the land simply to go fishing. But as the writer pointed out: 'they went to carry out their *malfeasance* by force, if necessary, of the deadliest kind … men do not go with guns to kill fish …' That is a much more interesting use of the term – the poachers going fishing was in itself unlawful, but they were charged with murder, and so they were guilty of *nonfeasance* in terms of their trespass for fishing, but also *misfeasance* perhaps, as they were not able to fish. Got that?

N

Necessaries: Traditionally, these items are the essential requisites for a child. These included drink, apparel, meat, drink and physic. By the Sale of Goods Act of 1893, these were 'goods suitable to the conditions of life for such an infant, and to his actual requirements ...' This may not seem so significant in law, but before that, a wife could pledge her husband's credit if she had to when 'necessaries' were urgent. This was abolished as recently as 1970.

Clearly, this business was an issue for the audience watching *The Importance of Being Earnest* when it was first performed at the St James' Theatre in 1895, because Algy was found in a handbag at a railway station, abandoned by a feckless romantic novelist. There were no necessaries in the bag at all, we understand.

Neifty: This is defined as 'the condition of being a serf.' Back in the twelfth and thirteenth centuries, the unfree members of society had a bad time. In fact, a powerful lord could imprison a man by licence of neifty. He was totally a possession of the Lord, who was his only heir. Another word, *sequela*, was used to describe the fruit of his loins, and the same word was used of pigs and cattle. That was the lot of the *neif*. The word *knave* relates to this.

Newgate: It would be fitting to use Dante's words here 'abandon all hope ye who enter here'. It was also known as 'the Whit' after Dick Whittington, the former Lord Mayor. It was an ancient place, called by some 'the prototype of Hell' and the 'bottomless pit of violence'. But if a prisoner happened to have some money with him, this 'rhino' could buy some comfort. In fact he could order anything he liked. The turnkeys lived by what they could force or cajole from their victims, a custom called 'garnish'.

Yet the place was hardly completely secure. The celebrated robber Jack Sheppard broke out of the place in 1724 even though he had been handcuffed, manacled and chained to the floor. Daniel Malden got out of the condemned cell and scuttled away through a sewer.

These adventures and the woeful tales of those who were to die at the end of the hangman's rope were in great demand, and the 'ordinaries' or keepers of the gaol made a handsome profit from selling these stories on broadsheets.

Of all the Newgate tales, the hangings are the most sensational. The condemned had to walk through Birdcage Walk to their doom, an alleyway under which bodies of former felons were interred. Waiting for the unfortunates outside by the scaffold were crowds of voyeurs. In 1807 thirty people were crushed during an execution 'show'.

Nominal damages: This refers to a trifling amount of money in a case in which, although the action is maintainable, the plaintiff has not really had any extreme damage done against him or her. One of the most famous examples is that of James McNeill Whistler, the artist, who sued the critic John Ruskin for libel. Ruskin had led a smear campaign against the Impressionist school of painters, and after looking at Whistler's painting 'Nocturne in Black and Gold' he wrote that he had 'never expected to hear a coxcomb ask two hundred guineas for flinging a pot of paint in the public's face'.

Whistler was asked in court if he really was asking such a huge sum for the work of just two days, and he answered 'No, it was for the knowledge gained through a lifetime'. The judge award one farthing damages and Whistler had to pay his costs of £500.

But this has its negative side, too, as in a case at the Old Bailey in 1990 when two youths were cleared of stealing two cans of lager worth £1.80 and the costs of the suit totalled £131,000.

Nonage (or nonagium): This referred to the ninth part of a person's movable possessions which used to be paid to the clergy on that person's death, but more often it was the 'absence of full age', so this was used to get young blades and fools out of various dilemmas in the past

In 1834, for instance, there was an action to recover the sum of £8 supplied to Lord Louth who was in debt to a tobacconist. The plaintiff was James Bacon. But Louth was a young nobleman who was away in Italy in 1834, and the alleged offence had been committed in 1828. As the brief for Mr Bacon said, 'Why had the tradesman waited five years?' The point was that the law said a person was liable to pay debts contracted during his minority. A witness was called to support the *nonage* of Louth at the time. All the fuss was over a meerschaum pipe.

Non sequitur: 'It does not follow'. This would apply perfectly to the barristers who indulged in tedious speeches and who annoyed the court by their eccentricities.

Notice to Treat: Clearly, this must mean that a certain person is to take another out shopping, or arrange for a wild party in celebration of the lucky one. In fact, it relates to compulsory land purchase. It is a notice given by an Act of 1845, to the poor victim whose land is about to be grabbed.

In the middle years of the nineteenth century, when the railway boom was in full swing, rail companies were serving notices to treat almost every week. But they met their match in 86-year-old Mrs Lipscomb in 1857. The company wanted to build over her land, which was at Liss in Hampshire, and in 1853 the firm agreed to pay the old lady £100 per acre, and they wanted to build on three acres. When they finally served the notice to treat in 1856 the land stated there was more than the three acres.

Mrs Lipscomb went to court and claimed money and damages, and also the right to take back her land. She won: the company's notice to treat was taken as an abandonment of the first agreement. The wine flowed freely that night at the Lipscombs' residence. The judge said that 'the company should not be embarrassed by the possibility of the trustees insisting on the agreement of 1853 …'

O

Obscenity: The Obscene Publications Acts of 1959 and 1964 defined 'obscene' as a product that would 'deprave or corrupt persons who are likely to read, see or hear the matter contained in it …'

Donald McGill was the artist who produced the famous 'saucy postcards' once found at all English seaside resorts. The humour of his cards was one of the treats of being on holiday and thousands of his cards were sent home by people who were relishing their time in the sun or in the pub. A typical card was one showing a scene in a bedroom in which a busty and scantily-clad blonde says to her lover, 'Blimey, here's my husband – can you come back tonight?' The man, looking suitably flushed and disturbed, is the stereotype milkman, and he replies, 'What, in my own ruddy time – are you kidding missus!'

But in the 1950s, McGill and his publishers were in trouble. The images and jokes were running into problems with the obscene publications legislation. He had experienced trouble before then, but not very often. McGill once said, with this trouble in mind, 'During the whole period of my career the authorities have made no complaints about the postcards drawn by me, with the following exceptions: in or about 1906 I recollect that an order was made for the destruction of a very large number of cards in the North of England; in or about 1920 proceedings were taken against the retailers of cards but no order was made'.

It comes as a shock to read about the problems in 1954, because McGill has the status of being recognised and complimented by no less a literary figure than George Orwell, who wrote an essay, *The Art of Donald McGill* in 1941, and in a letter to Anthony Powell in 1947 was well aware of the likelihood of offence caused by the cards when he said, 'Thanks so much for your postcard which I think was rather lucky to get here – at any rate I think the crofter who brings the post the last seven miles might have suppressed it if he had seen it'. He was living on the Isle of Jura, and he feared that the community there was too austere and morally righteous to accept the kind of ribald humour on a McGill card.

After the return to government of the Conservatives in 1951 there was a moral reaction to the slippage in 'standards' of morality in the arts as it was perceived at the time. In the five years following that date there were 167,000 books censored. It was only a matter of time before attention turned to the saucy postcard. At the time there were 'watch committees' at seaside resorts, and Cleethorpes was no exception. It was a regular occurrence to have complaints voiced against such things as the postcards, and many people considered them to be lewd rather than harmless fun. It was inevitable that there would be police raids on premises where cards might be in stock, and actions began to be taken in Grimsby. Police raids resulted in the arrest and prosecution of both publishers and artists.

The Grimsby County Petty Sessional Division court issued writs on behalf of the Director of Public Prosecutions against merchants who produced the McGill cards. The wording of the summons was 'unlawfully published an obscene postcard named Donald McGill Comics no. 811'. The Cleethorpes Chamber of Trade was worried too: in 1953 the Honorary Secretary wrote to Messrs D. Constance Ltd in London to find out about the circulation and distribution of the cards, because as the secretary wrote, 'seventeen shops in the town were raided by the police'. He added that 'Quantities of comic cards were taken away, so no doubt proceedings will follow to the annoyance to every one of the traders concerned'. He wanted to know if the cards in Cleethorpes were typical of the merchandise going elsewhere. Obviously, if there was a set range of cards going to every town, then there would be a massive number of raids and potential prosecutions.

This legal action stemmed from the 1857 Obscene Publications Act: the outcome locally was a prominent trial in Lincoln on 15 July 1954. McGill's own defence was that in most of the images he had 'no intention of double meaning and in fact in some cases, a 'double meaning' was pointed out to me ...' He was found guilty and had to pay £50 in a fine and £25 in costs. Obviously, large amounts of cards were destroyed; many of the smaller postcard producers were ruined.

The onslaught against publishers and shopkeepers was relentless: in Brighton in July 1953 magistrates ordered the destruction of 113 out of 175 varieties of postcards. One of the defendants spoke up on behalf of the general grievances felt by seaside traders when he said, 'You are a kind of arts council on this matter. When the Obscene Publications Act of 1857 was passed, England was worrying about Napoleon and standards of morality were lower than today' (he needed a history lesson). One merchant conceded that the cards were sometimes 'a little near the knuckle' but the most that could be said in criticism was that there was an innuendo in the image and the text.

At that time, people in Cleethorpes had been more worried by recent floods and extremely bad weather, but the affair certainly disturbed the normal equanimity of the Cleethorpes traders. As for George Orwell, he had his own defence of McGill:

The comic post cards are one expression of his point of view, a humble one, less important than the music halls, but still worthy of attention. In a society which is still basically Christian they naturally concentrate on sex jokes ... Their whole meaning and virtue is their unredeemed lowness. They stand for the worm's eye view of life ...

In other words, as with all humour of the baser kind, they remind us of the absurdity of moral strictness to the extent of denying communication about such topics as sex. But that view was too advanced for the austere world of 1950s Britain. With hindsight, it would be easy to see this case as a storm in a tea-cup – something rather more eccentric than important. But in fact the reasoning behind the bans was the significant factor. Here was a case in which a harmless and titivating ingredient of the English seaside experience was removed for the sake of 'decency', and of course today we are able to judge that in terms which seem unreal and distorted, because our modern political correctness has no room for what was then merely considered by most people to be 'saucy' in a way like the *Carry On* films.

But the McGill case turned out to be little more than yet another instance of what Lord Macaulay called, sarcastically, a 'fit of morality': 'We know of no spectacle so ridiculous as the British public in one of its periodical fits of morality'. Naturally, at the time it brought out yet again the debate about what is art and what is smut. Only six years after this fiasco Britain would have to cope with the attempt to understand the *Lady*

Chatterley's Lover trial. Like the McGill case, it would seem to many to be little more than victimisation on the part of the 'jobsworth'. Nevertheless, it is difficult today to bring to mind the kind of apprehensions felt by ordinary people, running their small businesses, in such a strange moral climate.

Oyez and terminer: In the days of the assizes, courts held across the land in the shires and presided over by traveling justices, the duties of the judges included the business of 'hearing and ending' cases and of 'gaol delivery' – concluding the cases involving the poor devils who had languished behind bars in the months before the court of the assize was finally held. Some of the sorting out of cases waiting decisions were horrendous, including death sentences of course. But there was a lighter side, as for instance in the *Castle Journal* report of a case at Carlisle in 1828:

> *The prisoner pleaded not guilty. The counsel for the prosecution being out of court, the judge called upon the witnesses, and was in the act of examining the first one, when Mr Peter Hodgson of Whitehaven, the attorney for the prosecution, came into court, and stopping the business, addressed his Lordship: 'My Lord, Mr Coltman, the counsel for the case, is at present engaged in another court.'*
> *JUDGE Well, I can't help that.*
> *HODSGON (after a pause) My Lord, shall I bring him here?*
> *JUDGE Don't interrupt me. Go and do your business. (Mr Hodgson's precipitate retreat occasioned a titter throughout the court).*

Petty treason (also called petit treason): This is a lower order of treason, the aim to kill or do harm to a sovereign, and in past times it could be committed by a servant killing his or her master; by a wife killing her husband, or by a churchman killing his superior, someone to whom he owed obedience. The clearest way to grasp the horrific consequences of such acts is to recall a case from the Georgian period.

Over the centuries, York Castle has witnessed some terrible scenes of human suffering, but few can equal the story of Elizabeth Broadingham. The narrative vaguely echoes the actions of Lady Macbeth 'lacking the 'milk of human kindness', except that the setting and the motives are the lowest and most despicable imaginable.

John Broadingham, her husband, was not exactly a pillar of the community. He was locked away in York dungeons for robbery when Elizabeth began her affair with Thomas Aikney, a younger man. It was a case of extreme passion, 'while the cat's away', and she liked the other man so much that she moved in with him.

A man coming out of prison after all kinds of deprivations expects some comfort and loyalty from his family. John Broadingham found none of this: he merely found that his wife had left the home. Elizabeth appears to have wanted more than simply living with Aikney as his partner; she wanted to be free of her marriage to John, and to remove the husband from the scene altogether was her aim. She began to work on Aikney with a view to leading him to murder John. The younger man at first resisted these pleas and wiles, but after some time he began to be influenced. It is recounted, though not definitely known, that Elizabeth made sure that Aikney had plenty of alcohol in him and tempted him in all the ways she could invent, to join a murderous pact. He finally went along with the plan.

Elizabeth must have been a very influential speaker and something of an actress; not only had she inveigled her way into Aikney's life, but she now also played the part of the good wife, returning to John and apparently wanting to restore the marital harmony they once had. John took her back. But only a week or so after moving back home, she was talking to Thomas Aikney about their plan, and sorting out the details of where and when it would be done. The lover still vainly tried to resist, but she was relentless. Poor Thomas thought that the best move was to run away and avoid the confrontation, to make a new start elsewhere.

Things came to a head on the night of 8 February 1776 when Elizabeth woke her husband as there was a loud noise downstairs; John staggered down to investigate and made his way to the door where Aikney was pounding on the wood. As John Broadingham opened up, Aikney knifed him in the chest and then, as the frenzied attack continued, he stabbed the man in the thigh and the leg. With the knife stuck in his belly, John managed to walk out into the street where he was seen by neighbours. So badly was the husband hurt that he had almost been eviscerated in the assault; he was clutching his stomach and his guts were exposed. The report at the time states that he was 'supporting his bowels'.

John Broadingham died the day after the attack. It took only a short time for neighbours and the magistrate to find Aikney and then the whole story was revealed. Elizabeth and Thomas confessed and he was hanged at York on 20 March. In this tale lies the incredible difference between punishment for murder and petty treason; Aikney's body, as was the custom, was cut down and then transported to Leeds Infirmary for use in dissection work for medical education. But Elizabeth had committed petty treason. Her fate was to be burnt at the stake. The only humane act in these cases was that the executioner normally strangled the woman before the fire was set alight, and he did so for Elizabeth. She was burnt and some ghoulish witnesses collected her ashes as souvenirs.

Mercy never entered into the matter when a woman was considered for the death penalty in the late eighteenth century and in the early nineteenth century. The great journalist of the period, J.W. Robertson Scott, has a memory of a woman on a scaffold at this time:

> *it was an old woman, a mere old wrinkled, wretched bundle. She was said to have killed a bastard. She cried, 'You cannot hang me!' But they did.*

Burning for petty treason, as explained in the introduction, was abolished in 1790: too late for Elizabeth Broadingham.

Y

Year and a day ruling: In the definition of murder in the classic legal documentation backing up statute law, the stipulation that a person had to die, after being attacked with murderous intent or with intent to cause grievous bodily harm, within a year and a day of the attack. This was an ancient ruling in common law, and the scope and applications of the law were always unclear. Lord Dormand commented as the move for its repeal was in progress: 'It certainly applies to murder, manslaughter, and aiding and abetting suicide ...'

This lasted until 1996. In previous periods, it made a lot of sense to have a period in which to ascertain motives if there was some complexity involved. But in recent times, with medical knowledge advancing so markedly, the maintenance of life in hospital by life-support machines left the ruling open to abuse and problems of interpretation.

The case of Ann Todd in Cottingham is an example of this being applied, though the case is unsolved. In 1901, in Cottingham, Hull, Ms Todd went to her door and was viciously attacked. She survived, but with very severe injuries. Then, on 1 February 1901, while staying with a relative in Anlaby Road, she died. The attack took place on 25 February 1900.

This case illustrates very well the way in which a reading of a court case adds immensely to our understanding of a prison sentence, and to the life of the condemned. The descriptions of the case, from the statements made by witnesses to the official indictments put before the magistrate and/or the court increase our knowledge of subsequent events in the life of the convicted person.

BIBLIOGRAPHY AND SOURCES

Note: Anyone writing on criminal records owes a huge debt to David T. Hawkings (see below). But since that book, there have been many advances in the provision of records online. However, for a full range of specimen texts from the records, Hawkings' volume has never been surpassed.

Before listing texts and sources, it is useful to have some notes on the range and nature of archival sources, especially those online, available to historians and researchers. I have presented these by category. Just as Sir Arthur Conan Doyle wrote of 'the manifold wickedness of the human heart' in his story *The Speckled Band,* so there are manifold sources concerning deviance and infamy through the centuries, and each has gathered its own library.

Every work cited and discussed is here; in the reference lists I have selected the volumes that apply most usefully to family history and social history research projects. I have also placed website details which have been mentioned in the texts under 'archives' or under 'websites'.

First steps
As a first search, it is difficult to beat the use of *The Times* Digital Archive and British Library Newspapers (extending up to 1950). These are available online and at your local library. I list them here under *Gengage*. After that, look at county record office listings online and, of course, databases such as those at Ancestry.co.uk or similar.

Using local sources
It may have become obvious in main text, but it needs to be said here that local sources are the starting point, and yet many of these will not relate directly to prison. Experience shows that a trawl across some set dates is

the most productive approach. This is time-consuming but may turn up something significant. A typical search might include:

- Quarter sessions/assizes records
- *Annual Register*
- Any available texts in record societies
- Press reports
- Convicts and transportation

More and more records are becoming available online, and often via Ancestry. An example of this is the completed *Convict Registers of Absolute Pardons 1791–1846* and the *New South Wales Certificates of Freedom 1827–1867*. What now opens up, online, is the material related to British transportations. As commentators have pointed out, from Ancestry's advertising, more than two million Britons have a convict ancestor in the records of convicts in Australia. The records of pardons and reprieves supply basic details such as ship boarded, occupation, physical features and date of journey/arrival.

Debtors

The family history magazines continue to provide very useful guides to specific topics, bringing together the most comprehensive sources. For debtors, I have referred to '6 Best websites for Tracing Debtors and Bankrupt Ancestors' in *Who Do You Think You Are?* magazine (7 October 2016). This is available online at www.whodoyouthinkyouaremagazine.com/6-best-websites-tracing-debtors-and-bankrupt-ancestors.

It is difficult to beat actual memoirs or biographies if the reader wishes to understand the life of a debtor in the days when debtors went to gaol. Any one of the many biographies of Charles Dickens will have a valuable account of the Marshalsea prison, as Dickens's father, John, was imprisoned there.

Mediaeval and Reformation period

There are very useful materials available in the online library guides of the Bodleian Library at Oxford. See https://libguides.bodleian.ox.ac.uk

These include mediaeval sources online, and a guide to reading cases in the rolls and records of the Elizabethan Star Chamber. Also, there are the common and piepowder courts of Southampton 1426–1483. For researchers who really want to delve into mediaeval records to find culprits and their destinies, the same site offers help for reading 'court hand' and shows example documents with transcriptions. The most formidable obstacle to accessing these records is the handwriting, along with the use of Latin. For many researchers, reliance has to be on the county record societies, whose invaluable work of translation and transcription goes on.

Bibliography

This listing is only an essential sample. For a more detailed bibliography, see my *Tracing Your Criminal Ancestors* (Pen and Sword, 2009). Note that the dates of first publication are shown in the first brackets. Here, I have mixed all categories, but every text mentioned in the text is listed first, regardless of the genre. The literature of crime is massive, and writings on prison history proliferate with every day that passes. I have found that with a good dictionary of law and the listings in a calendar of prisoners, much may be achieved.

Books referred to in the text

Baker, J.H., *An Introduction to English Legal History* (Butterworths, 2002)
Bamford, Samuel, *Passages in the Life of a Radical* (1884) (OUP, 1984)
Baring-Gould, S., *Yorkshire Oddities, Incidents and Strange Events* (1874) (Smith Settle, 1987)
Bede, *A History of the English Church and People* (731 AD) (Penguin, 1970)
Bidwell, George, *Forging his Chains* (S.S. Scranton and Co., 1888)
Brodsky, Joseph, *Less Than One* (1986) (Penguin, 2011)
Cadbury, Geraldine S., *Young Offenders, Yesterday and Today* (George Allen and Unwin, 1938)
Cooper, T.P., *The History of the Castle at York* (Elliot Stock, 1911)
Cyriax, Oliver, *The Penguin Encyclopaedia of Crime* (Penguin Books, 1996)
Davitt, Michael, *The Prison Life of Michael Davitt* (J.J. Lalor, 1882)
Eddleston, John J., *The Encyclopaedia of Executions* (John Blake, 2002)
Fitzherbert, Anthony, *La Novelle Natura Brevium* (1534) Available on the Project Gutenberg website: www.gutenberg.org.
Gibson, Charles B., *Life Among Convicts* (Hurst and Blackett, 1863)
Glazebrook, P.R., *Blackstones Statutes on Criminal Law 2009-2010* (OUP, 2010)
Godfrey, Barry, and Lawrence, Paul, *Crime and Justice 1750-1950* (Willan, 2005)
Gold, Claudia, *King of the North Wind* (William Collins, 2018)
Cox, Jane, *Hatred Pursued Beyond the Grave* (HMSO, 1993)
Gough, Richard, *The History of Myddle*, (Penguin, 1981)
Graeme-Evans, Alex, *A Short History Guide to Port Arthur 1830-77* (Regal Publications, 2001)

Greville, Charles, *A Journal of the reigns of King George IV, King William IV and Queen Victoria* (Longman Green, 1899)
Herber, Mark, *Legal London: A Pictorial History* (Phillimore, 1999)
Hirst, Joseph H., *The Blockhouses of Kingston-Upon-Hull* (A. Brown, 1913)
Howard, John, *The State of the Prisons* (J.M. Dent, 1929)
Knipe, William, *Criminal Chronology of York Castle* (Burdekin, 1867)
Louks, Nancy, *Prison Rules: A Working Guide* (Prison Reform Trust, 2000)
McCall, Andrew, *The Medieval Underworld* (Sutton, 2004)
Maxwell-Stewart, Hamish, and Hood, Susan, *Pack of Thieves?* (Port Arthur Historic Site, 2001)
Melling, Elizabeth, *Kentish Sources* (Kent County Council, 1969)
Mortimer, Ian, *The Time Traveller's Guide to Medieval England* (Bodley Head, 2008)
Paley, Ruth, and Fowler, Simon, *Family Skeletons* (National Archives, 2005)
Rutherford, Sarah, *The Victorian Asylum* (Shire, 2008)
Sandbach, J.B., *This Old Wig* (Right Book Club, 1949)
Satchell, Tony, *For Better or Worse* (Craftsman Press, 2003)
Stokes, Anthony, *Pit of Shame: The real ballad of Reading Gaol* (Waterside Press, 2007)
Stow, John, *A Survey of London written in the Year 1598* (Sutton, 2005)
Thomas, Donald R., *An Underworld at War* (The Murder Room, 2014)
Turbererville, A.S., *English Men and Manners in the Eighteenth Century* (OUP, 1926)
Wade, Stephen, *Lincolnshire Murders* (Sutton, 2006)
Wain, John, (Ed.) *The Journals of James Boswell 1761-1795* (Heinemann, 1991)
Younghusband, Sir George, *The Tower of London* (Herbert Jenkins, 1924)

Books: Reference
Bamford, Samuel, *Passages in the Life of a Radical* (OUP, 1984)
Brewer, Eberezer Cobham, (1870) *Wordsworth Dictionary of Phrase and Fable* (Wordsworth Editions, 2001)
Clarke, Tristram, *Tracing Your Scottish Ancestors: The Official Guide* (Birlinn, 1996)
Cook, Chris, *Britain in the Nineteenth Century 1815-1914* (Routledge, 2005)
Cowie, L.W., *The Wordsworth Dictionary of British Social History* (Wordsworth, 1973)
Friar, Stephen, *The Sutton Companion to Local History* (Sutton, 2001)
Godfrey, Barry, and Lawrence, Paul, *Crime and Justice 1750-1950* (Willan, 2005)

Griffiths, Major Arthur, *Mysteries of Police and Crime* (Cassell and Co., 1895)

Hawkings, David T., *Criminal Ancestors* (The History Press, 2009)

Herber, Mark, *Legal London* (Phillimore, 1999)

Hibbert, Christopher, *The Roots of Evil* (1963) (Sutton, 2003)

Hickey, D.J., and Doherty, J.E., *A New Dictionary of Irish History from 1800* (Gill and Macmillan, 2005)

Irving, Ronald, *The Law is an Ass* (Duckbacks, 2000)

Jusserand, J.J., *English wayfaring Life in the Middle Ages* (T. Fisher Unwin, 1899)

Powell, Vincent, *The Legal Companion* (Robson Books, 2005)

Priestley, Philip, *Victorian Prison Lives* (Pimlico, 1999)

Richardson, John, *The Local Historian's Encyclopaedia* (Historical Publications, 1974)

Saunders, John B., *Mozley & Whiteley's Law Dictionary* (Butterworth, 1977)

Scott, Sir Harold, *The Concise Encyclopaedia of Crime and Criminals* (Andre Deutsch, 1961)

Sinclair, Jenny, *A Walking Shadow: The remarkable double life of Edward Oxford* (Arcade Publications, 2012)

Contributions to books

Clanchy, M.T., 'Highway Robbery and Trial by Battle in the Hampshire Eyre of 1249' in R.F. Hunnisett & J.B. Post, *Medieval Legal Records* (HMSO: 1978)

James, M.E., 'The concept of order and the Northern Rising of 1569' in *Past and Present* No.60 August, 1973 pp.3-48

McConville, Sean, 'The Victorian Prison: England 1865-1965' in Morris, Norval and Rothman, David J., *The Oxford History of the Prison* (OUP, 1998) pp.117-150

Wade, Stephen, 'The Bite of Truth' in Edwards, Martin (Editor) *Truly Criminal* (The History Press, 2015) pp.270-273

Articles and Essays

Burn, Nigel, 'The Lincolnshire Poacher – 1201' *Lincolnshire Past and Present* No.102 Winter, 2015-16 p.11

Crotty, Homer D., 'The History of Insanity as a Defence to Crime in English Law' *California Law Review* 1924 See https://scholarship.law.berkleley.

Shoemaker, Robert, and Ward, Richard, 'Understanding the Criminal: Record-Keeping, Statistics and the early History of Criminology in England' *British Journal of Criminology Advance Access*, Sept. 19, 2016

Official Publications

Anon. *Cries from the Past: A History of Lincoln Castle Prison* (Jarrold, no date)

Anon. *Reports from the Commissioner, Inspectors and Others Session* 11 Feb., 896-Aug.1896 Vol. XXXIX: Part One, Lunacy: Holloway Sanatorium. (HMSO, 1896)

Further Correspondence on Discipline of Prisons in Her Majesty's Colonial Possessions (HMSO, 1868)

Harrison, Rachel Sponar, (Translator/editor) *Magna Carta of King John, AD 1215* (Lincoln castle Education and cultural services, no date)

Morrison, A.C.L., and Hughes, Edward, *The Criminal Justice Act, 1948* (Butterworth & Co., 1949)

Newman, P.R., *The Royal Castle of York* (York Castle Museum, no date)

Statutory Instrument 1964 No. 388 Prisons, England and Wales (HMSO, 1967)

Primary Archival Sources

The National Archives

For a full listing of all the prison sources at The National Archives, see David Hawkings' *Criminal Ancestors*, but this is a list of the most substantial sources:

Assizes: ASSI 21/20 also all ASSI references
Calendars: PCOM 2, HO 16, HO 77, HO 140 and CRIM 5
Hulks: see MIllbank registers at PCOM 2/2 and the PCOM references listed for regional gaols.
Journals: see PCOM 2 series listed online
Licences: see PCOM 3 and 5 series.
Old Bailey: all online but from 1834 when its jurisdiction was extended, the best reference is CRIM 1 for depositions and pardons.
Registers: PCOM 2 and MEPO 6
Transportation to America: the main references are at the Treasury collection: T1 class up to T53
Transportation to Australia: see HO 11, HO 17 and HO 31

Other archives

The following entries all relate to material quoted and discussed.

Gaol delivery: For this search, the National Archives reference is JUST 3- *Justices of Gaol Delivery: Gaol Delivery Rolls and Files.*

East Riding Archives
Champney Collection: DDX1361/2/53Qag 21 *Rules and regulations for the Government of the Beverley House of Correction* 1859
Qag ¼ Floor plan of the house of correction 1833
Qag 2 *Report of the Committee for the house of correction* 1819
Qag 14 *Return of the Establishment of Officers* 1833
Qag 5 *Annual return to the Secretary of State* 1823
Qag /21-34 *Specifications: a building for female prisoners* 1843
Quarter Sessions papers relating to the house of correction: DDX24/24

Lincoln County Archives
Brog 1 Lincoln Quarter Sessions, depositions and recognizances 4 May, 1869
Brog 1/4/4/1/6 Records of indictments
Brog 1/5/2/1 Annual return of Lunatics chargeable to the Common Fund of the Lincoln Union
Co.C.2/7 Gaol Sessions 3 June, 1870
G.H. 1/18 Lincolnshire Girls' Home miscellaneous documents and admission registers 1870-1910
H 10/1 Indenture
Hancock 3:
Lincoln Prison 1 Nominal Record 1877-1879
Return for Lincoln City Prison 1878

Other archival sources
Gaol Keeper's Journal 1833-38 Huntingdon County gaol HCP/2/320/1 Huntingdon County Record Office.

Liverpool Catholic Reformatory Association Ref. 364CAT, See https:// discovery.nationalarchives.gov.uk

London Metropolitan Archives See www.cityoflondon.gov.uk . Also the linked site, www.londonlives.org. The leaflet- *Information Leaflet no. 59 Prison Records* is particularly useful.

Northern Ireland
www.findmypast.co.uk/articles/world-records/full-list-of-the-irish-family-history-records
PRONI: www.nidirect.gov.uk>proni

Parliamentary papers and reports
Note: A perusal of the bound volumes is recommended, and a visit to a library holding a set of the papers will be most rewarding.
See https://libguides.bodleian.ox.ac.uk/parliament/1800-2000
Police Gazette: see: www.britishnewspaperarchive.c.uk/titles/police-gazette
Rolls of Parliament Vol.ii pp.9, 12 1 Ed.III A.D.1326-7

Some specific reports available in print will show the nature of these as sources:

Report of the Directors of Convict Prisoners on the Discvipline and Management of Pentonville, Millbank and Parkhurst 2018
Anon. *Return of the Number of Prisoners on 1st May, 1861 in Brixton, Chatham, Dartmoor, Fulham, Millbank, Parkhurst.* (1861)
Anon. *Report of the Committee on Insanity and Crime* (HMSO 1924)

Prison Service
Instructions to Governors IG38/1995 Record management

Statutory Instruments: Prison Rules
The Prison Rules traditionally govern everyday activities in the regime. To understand the regime your ancestor experienced, a look at the Statutory Instruments for these rules is very enlightening. For instance, the rules issued in 1964 are: *Statutory Instruments 1964 No. 388 Prisons: England and Wales. The Prison Rules 1964* (HMSO, 1964)

Scottish Records
www.glasgowfamilyhistory.org.uk
www.scan.org.uk/familyhistory/myancestors/prisoner.htm
www.scottishindexes.com>learningprison

West Yorkshire Archives
www.ancestry.co.uk/search/collections/westyorkprison/ The women's records quoted are here.

Archival Material in Print
Annual Register. See https://onlinebooks.library.upenn.edu
Hanawalt, Barbara, (Ed.) *Crime in East Anglia: Norfolk Gaol Delivery Rolls 1307–1316* (Norfolk Record Society, 1970)
Parliamentary papers/state trials: see for instance Thomas, Donald (Ed.) *State Trials* (2 volumes) (Routledge and Kegan Paul, 1972)

Quarter Sessions Records of the West Riding
Indictment Book for 1637 (Yorkshire Archaeological Society, 1915)
Quarter Sessions Records of the West Riding 1645 (Yorkshire Archaeological Society, 1915)

The Surtees Society
The Surtees Society was formed in 1834, with Robert Surtees of Mainforth as the central figure. His work *The History and Antiquities of the County Palatinate of Durham (1816-1840)* is a formative volume. The Society published works relating to the history of Northumberland and Durham, and many of the publications relate to courts and imprisonment. These are examples:

Durham Quarter Sessions Rolls 1471–1625
The Justicing Notebook of Edmund Tew, Rector of Bolden (1750–1764)
Northumberland Eyre Roll for 1293

These are all published for the Society by Boydell and Brewer. See: www.surteessocirty.org.uk and https://boydellandbrewer.com

Unpublished works
Lange, Mary, *The Search for John Calvert or the 'convict who disappeared from view'*, 1992 Local Studies Collection, East Riding Archives.
Tobia, Paul, *The Patients of the Bristol Lunatic Asylum in the Nineteenth Century 1861-1900* Doctoral thesis, March, 2017 see *eprints.uwe.ac.uk*

Websites
www.bbc.co.uk/whodoyouthinkyouare/past-stories/john-hurt.shtml The John Hurt story is here.
www.blacksheepancestors.com/uk/prisons This is one of the most productive and informative resources sites for prison history, and it also has lists of inmates for some particular years. Prisons covered for prisoner lists are: Brixton, 1871; Pentonville, 1881; Canterbury, 1901; Woking Invalid prison, 1881; Aylesbury, 1870; Wormwood Scrubs, 1881; Millbank, 1881; Wakefield, 1891. There are also some lists of convict prisoners sailing from UK to Australia between 1788 and 1791.

In addition, there are prison histories and accounts of famous cases.

www.british-history.ac.uk
www.digitalpanopticon.org

The Gengage group: *The Times Digital Archive* and *British Library Newspapers* (to 1950)

www.glasgowfamilyhistory.org.uk

www.itsaboutlincoln.co.uk>the-stonebow-guildhall

www.oxforddnb.com/vuiew/1093 This has the quoted biography of Edmund Du Cane by Bill Forsythe.

www.prisonhistory.org>prison>lincoln-borough-gaol

www.scottishindexes.com>7;earningprison

www.thegazette.co.uk This contains the history of the Gazette and more information on the history and development of its issues and subjects.

www://hansard.millbanksystems.com/written_answers/1967 This has the case of the teenager mentioned in the introduction. The *Gazette* is online and accessible for free.

https://doncasterhistory.wordpress.com/local/history

www.yas.org.uk The most useful resource here, on the Yorkshire Archaeological Society's lists of York prisoners and on West Riding Quarter Sessions, is the online year-by-year list of subjects covered through Victorian and Edwardian periods.

Periodicals and newspapers

The process of assembling information on a criminal life from the past entails a determined search of all official publications, and this list could be very long. But it is always surprising where names may be found and more material added to the ancestor's life. A perfect instance of this is the Victorian *Police Gazette* (previously *Hue and Cry*) which listed names and descriptions of wanted people, and also lists of army deserters.

As an example, the issue for 11 November 1829 includes a list of fifty-six army deserters, with a full physical description of each man. The information even includes parish, corps, county, trade and very detailed facial descriptions. It also lists names of persons charged at the London police offices, so if the researcher woks 'backwards' from a known prison sentence, then the first charge by police may be found.

The Police Gazette

This is dispersed over many different repositories, and the difficulty in using these for tracing an ancestor lies in the fact that for various runs of years, they are in print, but some will be in London, and others in a dozen different county archives. But the most substantial are:

The British Library Newspaper Library, Colindale Avenue, London NW9 5HE. These cover the years 1801; 1802; 1815; 1818-1834; 1877–1900.

Metropolitan Police Museum, New Scotland Yard, London. These cover the years 1793; 1816; 1831; 1832;1838; 1842; 1845; 1878.

Ephemera
Although these items are often hard to find, they are there in archives as a rule, and the material they supply is invaluable for gathering secondary information about a prisoner and/or about the prison they were held in. Many of these are small-scale local publications such as almanacs, press cuttings or self-published works. The following are the ones mentioned and discussed in the above pages.

Anon. *The Strangeways Murder* (Sporting News. Manchester, no date) Reprinted by Clifford Elmer, Cheadle: 2004)
Fullbrook, Edward, *Illustrated letter* (Ken Spelman catalogue of mss. 2019)

Transportation: bibliographical guide
There has been such a boom in the growth in materials available for research into convict lives, that it is worthwhile having a separate short guide to the main texts available. At the centre is David Hawkings' *Bound for Australia* (Phillimore, 1987). This gives an account of the series of events and actions in the trajectory of a convict life. The appendix has a collection of source documents.

The other solid, invaluable volume on the subject is surely Charles Bateson's *The Convict Ships 1787-1868*, (Brown, Son & Ferguson, 1959) This is essential for any research into convict ancestors, even having lists of such people as surgeons and ships' masters. The material here is particularly useful on the management and administration of the ships and voyages.

As an example of a guide to specific elements in the system, we have John Clay's Maconochie's Experiment (John Murray, 2001) which explains the significance of Governor Maconochie's systems of 'marks' for convicts. This was a method of logging good behaviour and shaving off time from convicts' sentences.

Other useful books:

Baker, A.W., *Death is a Good Solution: the convict experience in early Australia* (University of Queensland Press, 1984)
Beattie, J.W., *Port Arthur* (Port Arthur Museum, no date)
Cobley, John, *The Crimes of the First Fleet Convicts* (Angus and Robertson, 1970)

Easty, John, *Memorandum of the Transactions of a Voyage from England to Botany Bay 1787-1793* (Public Library of New South Wales, 1965)

Keneally, Tom, *The Commonwealth of Thieves* (Chatto and Windus, 2006)

King, Jonathan, *The First Settlement: the convict village that founded Australia* (Macmillan Australia, 1984)

Timeline of Prison History

1115   The first true prison on record: the baulk house at Winchester.
1165   Bedford prison established.
1166   The Assize of Clarendon directed that where there are no gaols, sheriffs are to construct them.
1275   Statute of Westminster.
1332   Hexham gaol completed and opened.
1361   The first justices of the peace.
1423   The first version of Newgate prison erected, funded by Richard Whittington.
1450   First recorded use of the Tower rack.
1485   The Court of Star Chamber created.
1534   Treason Act (building on the 1351 Act).
1555   The first house of correction established, at Bridewell, Blackfriars.
1576   An Act to establish houses of correction across the land.
1597   An Act for establishing workhouses for the poor passed.
1686   Last hanging for witchcraft in England – that of Alice Molland.
1714   Vagrancy Act: first statute to provide for the detention of lunatics.
1735   The Witchcraft Act repeals the death penalty for witchcraft.
1744   The Madhouse Act: made licences for private madhouses in the London area.
1777   John Howard published *The State of the Prisons*, a survey and critique of all local gaols.
1788   The arrival of the first fleet of transported convicts in Botany Bay.
1790   Abolition of burning of women in England for petty treason.
1791   Jeremy Bentham proposes his idea for a penitentiary.
1800   Criminal Lunatics Act: medical supervision made a legal requirement.
1811   The Select Committee on Penitentiary Houses recommends a penitentiary be built at Millbank (the current site of Tate Modern).
1814   Abolition of beheading.
1817   The last recorded public flogging of a woman in England.
1820   The flogging of women prisoners is abolished.
1830s The 'Silent System' introduced.
1832   Abolition of dissection after hanging.

1834	Abolition of gibbeting in England.
1843	The Millbank experiment fails: the prison is closed.
1856	The first recommendation that hanging is done in private, inside the walls.
1863	The Carnarvon Committee recommends a regime more attuned to punishment. Broadmoor opened as Broadmoor Criminal Lunatic Asylum.
1867	The end of convict transportation.
1868	Hanging is made private.
1879	Abolition of branding as a punishment.
1895	The Departmental Committee on Prisons indicates that there should be another switch, from a stress on punishment to an investment in rehabilitation.
1898	The crank and the treadmill were finally abolished.
1907	The establishment of a Court of Criminal Appeal. The first professional probation service created.
1908	The Borstal Act establishes the first juvenile offenders' scheme with the new ideas of a standardised regime in place. This was for people aged between sixteen and twenty-one.
1917	Dartmoor receives over a thousand 'conscientious objectors'.
1932	Mutiny at Dartmoor.
1946	A serious mutiny at Northallerton prison.
1948	Military drill introduced at detention centres.
1976	Serious riot at HMP Hull.
1983	Charles Bronson stages a rooftop protest at Broadmoor.
1990	Riots in Dartmoor.
1991	The Criminal Justice Act: 'integral sanitation' introduced. In other words, 'slopping out' ended.
1995	Ronnie Kray dies.
1999	Charles Bronson takes an education officer hostage at HMP Hull.
2000	Reggie Kray is released from prison on compassionate grounds, and dies a few weeks after release.
2007	'The Istanbul Statement' puts forward the guideline that solitary confinement should be prohibited for death row prisoners and life-sentenced prisoners, for mentally ill prisoners and children under eighteen.

INDEX

Annual Register, 118–19
Assize of Clarendon (1166), 1
Assizes, 2, 9–10
Athelstan, 99

Baker, J.H., 55
Bamford, Samuel, xix
   Passages in the Life of a Radical, xix
Bankrupt Directory, 45
Baring-Gould, Sabine, 86
Beccaria, Cesare, xvii
Beverley House of Correction, 22–4
'Bloody Code', 40
Borstals, 101–103
Bridewells, 15
Broadmoor, 91–2

Calendars of prisoners, 37–8
Calendars of State Prisoners, 11
Church courts, 7
Clackclose, 2–3
Clanchy, M.T., 3
Court of Criminal Appeal, viii
Court records, 40–1
Cyriax, Oliver, 1

Davitt, Michael, 109–11
Debtors' Prisons, 42–5
Delivery Rolls, 6
Digital Panopticaon, 82
Du Cane, Edmund, 63–4
Dunhill family, 86–8

Edward I, 10
Edward II, 5
Embezzlement, 54–5
Enlightenment, the, xvi
Ephemera, 172
Evangelical Alliance, xii
Evelyn, John, xv
Eyres, 2

Female Life in Prison, 76
Fitzherbert, Anthony, 90
Francis, John, 96–7

Game Laws, 75
Gaol Acts (1820s), 13, 17
Garrett, H.G., 55
George III, 90
Gloucestershire Penitentiary, 17–18
Gold, Claudia, 11
Goudie fraud (Liverpool), 11
Gough, Richard, 15
   The History of Myddle, 15
   Governors, 16
Greville, Charles, 21

Habitual Offenders Act (!869), 52
Heath, Neville, 103
Holmes, Thomas, 57–9
Home Office, 6, 124
Houses of Correction, 16–9
Howard, John, 15, 20–2
Huggins State Trial, 106–108

Hulks (prison ships), 83–4
Huntingdon County Gaol, 17
Hurt, John, 54

Jebb, Joshua, 92
Johnson, Dr Samuel, 115
Justicia (hulk), 85

Lamb, Charles, 92
Lincoln Prison (Georgian) xx
London prison records, 115–17
Luddite Risings, ix
Lunatics, criminal, 89–93

McCall, Andrew, 7
McConville, Sean, 39
Maclean, Roderick, 94–5
Magna Carta, 4
Maidstone Gaol, 17–18
Mayhew, Henry and Binny, John, 19–20, 26
   The Criminal Prisons of London, 19
Mayflower pilgrims, xi
Memoirs, 109–11
Militia, 20
Monastic gaols, 7

Nisi Prius (court), 10
Norfolk Record Society, 2
Northallerton Prison, 30–5, 65–6
Northern Ireland Records, 71–2
Norwich Castle, 2

Old Bailey, 76
Oglethorpe, John, 76
Old Bailey Sessions Papers, 113–15
Order books, 42
Oxford, Edward, 96
Oyez and terminez, 2

Paul, Sir George Onisiphorous, xvii
Peel, Sir Robert, 35, 40

Penitentiaries, 39
Peterborough Abbey, 9
Pipe Rolls, 6
Police Court Missionaries, 57–61
Police Gazette, 120–2
Prevention of Crime Act (1908), 52
Prison Books and Journals 68–9
Prisons Act (1878), 63
Prison work, 28–9
Proceedings in Courts of Justice Act (1731), 3

Quarter Sessions, 36

Reading Gaol, 74
Reformatories, 101
Returns of Prisoners, 51

Scottish records, 70–2
Staff in prisons, 29–30
Stow, John, 15
Stow (Lincs), 6
Suffragettes, xiii
Surrey Asylum, 18

Thames Police Court, 18
Ticket of Leave, 53
Tower of London, 116
Transportation, 75–82
Transportation probationary system, 78
Treadmill, 33–4

Victoria, Queen, 94

Wesley, Samuel, 46–9
Wilde, Oscar, 72–4
Women's Prisons, 67–9

York Castle, 11–14
Young Offenders, 99–101